Canyon Diablo

by

Zeke Crandall

In memory of Buckey O'Neill

Zeke Crandall

This book is published by Zeke Crandall 6210 West Shaw Butte Drive, Glendale, Arizona 85304

All rights to this book in any form are strictly prohibited unless authorized by the author2012 with all copyrights reserved.

The ISBN number is 978-0-9773784-6-3 and the book's copyright number through the United States Library of Congress is TXu0018130-80

Soft bound copies of Canyon Diablo, are Available for sale at discounted internet pricing on our website www.arizonatales.com or by email, my email addressis zekecrandall46@hotmail.com.

The cover photo is courtesy of Leo Boudreau along with and Underwood & Underwood the original copyright owners of the picture.

Other published soft bound books that are Currently available by this author are, Arizona Tales, Arizona Train Robbers, The Simple Man, Ghost in the Desert, and The Power Affair, all through our website or email.

Look for new books written by this author as well as new books on Kindle and hard copy over 2016-2018 including, The Death Cave, Tonto Basin Pioneer, Pleasant Valley Revisited, Arizona Tales Vol 2, The Camel Project and Boxing Referee.

Thank you,
Zeke Crandall

Preface

The author has lived in Arizona since the age of nine and arrived in Arizona 1955, Mom lived in Prescott for fifteen years before passing in December of 2014. Prescott, Arizona, is located in Yavapai County, a short 90 miles north from our home in Glendale. Like most of us though, I have marveled at the beautiful statue dedicated to "Buckey" O'Neill that is located in front of Prescott's Courthouse, in the center of town.

The only facts I knew about William Owen "Buckey" O'Neill before researching for this book, was that he was a Rough Rider. He was killed during the Spanish-American War in 1898, and was loved by Colonel Theodore Roosevelt, who said:

> "The greatest loss America endured in the Spanish-American war was the death of Lieutenant William Owen Buckey O'Neill."

While walking around the Courthouse Square lawn park one morning, I stopped to read the dedication wording on the Rough Rider statue. I decided right then and there that I wanted to know more about this great man. I soon realized after spending many timeless hours at Sharlot Hall Museum reading every newspaper article, magazine article and the book written by Dan Taylor about Buckey O'Neill's life, that I needed to bring him back to life for all Americans.

Sharlot Hall Museum is a true Arizona Treasure. Besides recently adding a beautiful new archives building to the museum, they have a building dedicated to the History of Northern Arizona that includes videos with five separate areas, one of which is dedicated to Arizona's Indian population. The museum grounds include the first territorial governor's mansion *(original location)*, as well as other buildings that were built duplicating the craftsmanship from the territorial era.

Prescott has many historical places a traveler can visit. Including, but not limited to, Yavapai Hills where Tom Mix filmed over 200 movies, Granite Dells, Arizona's Territorial Courthouse and the park that surrounds it, The Hotel St. Michael and Whiskey Row. The immediate surrounding streets of the Courthouse Square are Gurley, Cortez, Montezuma, and Goodwin. Around this square and radiating out, is a plethora of specialty shopping boutiques, eating establishments, saloons, and the Bashford Court stores.

In the early years, the founding fathers and business owners of the Town of Prescott knew they wanted the revenue from the 24-hour-a-day activities of the more than 100 saloons, gambling establishments, dance halls and brothels, so they centralized all of these types of businesses into a two-block area on Montezuma Street, calling it, "Whiskey Row." The owners of the business, their families, children, tourists and God fearing folks were able to stay clear of the seedy area, as the establishment owners wanted to capitalize on the 24 hour 7 day a week revenue these businesses generated. Thank you Jeff Foreman for editing and Joe Schuler, for help with covers.

This photo of the statue of "Buckey," and the plaque that is placed below the statue with the dedication wording was taken by author

Chapter One

With our love of the Old West and its characters, one must not forget the name and deeds of William Owen "Buckey" O'Neill and his thrilling life. Our hearts are still grateful for the Rough Riders who died gallantly in Cuba, fighting in the Spanish-American war at the turn of the 19th Century, but none more than William "Buckey" O'Neill, who always had a smile on his face and a cigar in his mouth.

He will be remembered as a fearless leader of men in a new wild country where only the strong survive. He was a complex as well an aggressive man. He was a newspaper reporter, editor, lawyer, judge, sheriff, politician, and lastly a gallant soldier who gave his life fighting for freedom, which is the basic American belief that was established by our forefathers in the Constitution of the United States of America. He was one of the greatest American heroes to hail from the great state of Arizona.

William Owen Buckey O'Neill was a strange mixture of temperaments, a blend of adventure and the son of a civilization that lent "Buckey" his peculiar charm. He was college educated, a student of the classics and best literature of the day. But this same man, who quoted Walt Whitman in the heat of battle as his troops began the assault of San-Juan Hill during the war in Cuba, while bullets spattered all around him, earned his nickname of Buckey by his reckless plunging in the gambling houses of Arizona where Mexicans, Chinamen, Native Americans, tourists, cowpunchers, ranchers, miners and desperados rubbed shoulders at the Faro and Poker tables.

William Owen O'Neill received his nickname Buckey, gambling at the Faro tables at The Palace Bar on Whiskey Row in Prescott, Arizona. The game of Faro was also called "Bucking the Tiger." Because of William's tenacity and recklessness at the Faro tables, along with spending a lot of his free time gambling, he was given the nickname, Buckey, that stuck with him for the rest of his life.

Below is a picture found in the National Archives of the Palace Bar, Prescott, Arizona, circa 1890.

The outstanding note of Buckey O'Neill was his vitality, the amazing energy of his manhood. He could do foolish, prodigal things, but it was not in him to be mean. He had soft brown eyes, black hair, a friendly smile, always greeting the stranger who chanced by him. He was a tiger in spirit, but he had a graceful, respectful inner power that only surfaced when it was needed. His was a soft-spoken young man. One would wait long before hearing from him that he was one of the most famous, dramatic daredevil's in the Old West. Like a flash of lightning when the call to action came, he hadn't a word to say for himself after the crisis had been met and was past.

Buckey O'Neill had a great sense of recklessness, humor and generosity in always doing the right thing. The Atlantic & Pacific Railroad was building a rail line through Yavapai County when he was the newly elected county sheriff. As it was reported by the Coconino Sun Newspaper, one of the construction gangs confiscated a spring that belonged to the Navajo Indian Tribe. The Navajo people were peaceful farmers and sheepherders. They submitted to the injustice but their sheep began to perish for lack of water.

Sheriff O'Neill heard about their predicament, he flung a saddle over his horse and rode across the county to the place where the train gang of graders was at work. He explained to the foreman of the outfit that they would have to restore the spring to its rightful owners. The foreman was a very big Irishman who looked down at the gentle-eyed, soft spoken sheriff and announced loudly so all of his crew could hear,

> "You better go home to your mother sonny."

Obviously boiling inside, but showing no emotion, the young sheriff kept his composure and looked up at the big fellow and simply said to him,

> "You will give them back their spring."

The foreman hollered back at Buckey,

> "Make us buckaroo."

Buckey answered back,

> "Just as you say sir but you will return the spring to its rightful owners one way or another."

The young sheriff tipped his hat and said goodbye to the railroad grading gang. He wished them a good day and proceeded to tell the foreman,

> "I'll be back."

Sheriff O'Neill rode directly to the nearby Navajo village and after explaining his plan to the chief, armed the chief and twenty-five of his braves with rifles and swore them in as his special deputies. He then led the posse of Navajo braves back to where the railroad grading camp was located as suggested earlier by the foreman.

Sheriff O'Neill and his deputies surrounded the men at their camp the next morning at which time the young sheriff approached the foreman. He simply looked at the big Irishman and said,

> "Good morning fellas! I'm back!" "You have two choices. The first one is that we can fight it out. The second choice and a better one is to move your camp and give the spring back to its rightful owners!"

The foreman and his men decided it would be best to move on and restore the spring to the

Navajo village. The Navajo chief, Hosteen Redshirt, was so impressed with Sheriff O'Neill's bravery and grit, he presented Buckey with a silver and turquoise ring.

This occasion was not the only time that the young sheriff came in conflict with the railroad. One of his campaign promises when he ran for the office of Sheriff of Yavapai County in November of 1888, if elected, was to assess the railroads the full value of their land holdings in the county. This amounted to every section of land they owned on both sides of the railroad tracks that ran through Yavapai County. The Atlantic & Pacific Railroad was estimated to own over seven hundred sections alone just in Yavapai County. Besides being responsible for keeping the peace, the county sheriff's office also doubled as the county tax assessor. This issue ended up being the sole issue of his campaign and was bitterly fought by the Atlantic & Pacific Railroad.

A couple of weeks after O'Neill won the election for the Sheriff of Yavapai County the Atlantic & Pacific Railroad soon realized they were going to have to pay the land assessment for their vast holdings in the county. So they sent representatives to Prescott to meet with the newly elected Sheriff O'Neill to negotiate a viable settlement that would be acceptable to both parties.

Sheriff O'Neill knew there was no way the railroad was going to pay land taxes on the large acreage they owned so he and the railroad worked out a settlement that in short,

"If the county was called by the railroad to pursue any outlaws that robbed a train in Yavapai County, the railroad would be responsible for paying all expenses incurred by the county sheriff officer's posse in the pursuit, capture and trial of the outlaws."

Chapter Two

In this chapter the author will present a brief history of train robberies and train robbers to familiarize the reader with the problem nationally, along with train robbing here in the Territory of Arizona. In this book, the focus is the Canyon Diablo Train Robbery on March 20, 1899, that was carried by every newspaper in the east and brought national attention to Arizona and the newly elected Yavapai County Sheriff Buckey O'Neill. It was one of the most spectacular pursuits in the history of Arizona as well as making a national hero out of Sheriff O'Neill who went on to be one of the greatest men in Arizona History.

Although trains had been moving goods and people back and forth across the eastern United States for much of the first half of the 1800's; the first non-wartime train robbery occurred on October 6, 1866, outside Seymour, Indiana. As the train pulled out of the Seymour Station that evening, two of the Reno brothers quietly boarded the express car, stepped inside, and aimed their revolvers at the messenger. Within fifteen minutes, they had emptied one of the two safes on board, pushed the other safe out the door, and hopped off the train. Lawmen nabbed the perpetrators four days later and the $40,000 taken from the robbery. Another robbery occurred on October 6, 1866 near Bristow, Kentucky. In this case, robbers derailed an L & N Train. As the stunned crew scrambled from the wreckage, the bandits forced their way into the Wells Fargo car and stole $8,000. A few weeks later, bandits used a pile of wood to wreck a passenger train carrying a U.S. Government payroll near Franklin, Kentucky. Masked men robbed passengers and the Wells Fargo car.

The Seymour train robbery did not receive much attention, but the Kentucky train heists were highly publicized, indicating how easy it was to hold up a train. They also demonstrated the ease and effectiveness of wrecking a train in order to rob it. Railroad officials throughout the country were horrified at the potential loss of life and property that might accompany an epidemic of train robbing. As one historian wrote these train robberies launched a fifty-year battle between railroads and train robberies and the battle eventually spilled over into Arizona.

The Arizona train robberies, as well as the rest of the west, were considered extensions of the stage robberies that preceded them. A recent compilation documents 129 successful stage holdups in the territory between 1875 and 1903; ninety-nine of these occurred prior to 1890. Aside from 1894, when there were seven heists, stage holdups in Arizona became increasingly rare. Two factors contributed to the decline. First of all, the Wells Fargo Company, the principle messenger service in Arizona, became more protective of its shipments.

The express company offered a standard $300 reward for the capture of anyone, who robbed one of their train cars, and they armed its baggage car messengers to help supplement the local law enforcement agencies and they also maintained a staff of railroad detectives and special officers to hunt down stage robbers. While less than half of the Arizona stage holdups went unsolved, not all of the robberies involved Wells Fargo shipments. Wells Fargo historians say that of their shipments that were stolen in Arizona, most of the perpetrators, were apprehended.

A second, more important, factor contributing to the decline of stage holdups was the simple fact that fewer and fewer stagecoaches carried valuable shipments. Stage robberies had all but disappeared nationwide by the 1890s. In fact, the Wells Fargo Company records indicate that in 1887 the average haul per stage robbery was a lowly $20. Arizona mirrored this national trend as its railroad network matured and expanded after the decade of the 1880's. It was very simple, the loot was on the trains and stagecoaches were not worth the risk.

By 1887 two transcontinental railroads completely traversed Arizona. The Southern Pacific was the first and arrived at Yuma from California in 1877 and from there passed though Tucson finally reaching the Arizona/New Mexico border in 1880. It then connected with the Texas Pacific Railroad a little east of El Paso. The main trunk and its various feeder lines solidified Tucson's role as a commercial center and helped fuel the Salt River Valley's already substantial growth as an agricultural oasis.

A second railroad, originally chartered by the A & P, short for the Atlantic & Pacific, *(that later became the Southern Pacific)* traversed northern Arizona by 1883, stimulating the first substantial non-Indian settlements in the small towns it passed. Knowing the railroad would soon be passing through, by 1880, ranchers and farmers began to relocate into the north, eastern and central parts of Yavapai County, near or around the Trans-America railroad line that was located about ninety miles north of Prescott, Arizona.

One of the main cities along the northern railroad route that became a hub for freight was Flagstaff. Soon after the rails arrived there in 1882, cattle cars began bringing in thousands of head of livestock to graze on the unclaimed ranges of northern Arizona. In addition, as the railroad wound its way through the northern forests, it created both a market for and transportation of the readily available timber and thus fueled a logging industry. By transporting ore more cost-effectively than freight wagons, railroads and their feeder lines also stimulated huge growth in copper mining. The northern part of Yavapai county brought economic opportunities for thousands of new comers arriving by the droves to Arizona, dramatically changing our territorial society, but sadly also opening up new avenues for crime.

One of the last sensational train robberies on the Southern Pacific line in Arizona, occurred on the night of April 27, 1887, eighteen miles east of Tucson. A gang of eight outlaws waved a red lantern; commonly used by train robbers throughout the United States, signaling for the engineer to stop the train. Obstructions on the track further up the line provided a backup in case the train crew ignored the signal.

The train halted, but the Wells Fargo messenger, Charles F. Smith, refused to open the express car. While the robbers attempted to pry open the door, Smith hid $3,500 in gold in the stove. Finally, the holdup men set a black powder charge and threatened to blow open the door. Smith, fearing he would be blown up as well, opened the door to allow the robbers to enter, and hoping they would not discover that he had the gold and where he hid it.

The masked outlaws took control of the locomotive and they uncoupled the postal, baggage and express cars from the rest of the train. They left the passengers sitting in the cars, while the locomotive pulled forward about six miles with the three cars in tow. There, the robbers ransacked the mail and express packages and made off with about $3,200. One of the outlaws knew how to operate a locomotive, causing most observers and lawmen to believe that the robbery could well have been an inside job, or at least it was perpetrated by current or former railroad employees. Suspects were arrested a few weeks later, but were released when they provided valid alibis and had nothing from the heist on them when they were questioned.

On August 10th the same train was hit about one mile east of the site of the first robbery. The robbers once again attempted the red lantern trick. This time, however, the engineer was unable to stop in time. The locomotive thundered into an open switch, causing it to derail and tip over. A few passengers were hurt, but fortunately no one was killed. When Charles Smith, the same express employee, who was on duty as the Wells Fargo Messenger, once again stubbornly refused to open the express car, the impatient bandits went ahead and blew a hole in the door. As two of the men entered the car, one of them who obviously knew the messenger reportedly said,

"Smitty, the stove racket won't deter us this time. You're still obstinate, huh."

Smith refused to unlock the safe until he had been hit on the head a few time with a revolver. Although no official amount was reported, the robbers were thought to have made off with about $2,000. Five of the men were arrested for the crime but only two were convicted and served time.

A third robbery along the southern line occurred on February 22, 1888, when two masked men sneaked aboard a train as it pulled from the station near Stein's Pass on the border between New Mexico and Arizona. A mile and a half down the tack, they ordered the engineer to stop, forced the messenger to open the express car, and fled with about $700.

Train robberies did not start in northern Arizona until September 16, 1887. Robbers set a bonfire in the middle of the tracks of the Atlantic & Pacific eastbound passenger train near Navajo Springs. As the train pulled to a halt, a shot was fired at the locomotive cab while another was directed at the conductor. Five masked men boarded the train and then proceeded to steal a small safe from the express car and rode off into the night, leaving behind more contents in a larger safe that had been rerouted from San Francisco.

A second heist took place along the same line of the A & P Railroad on September 8, 1888, near the Bellemont Station just west of Flagstaff. Three masked highwaymen unhitched the locomotive and one car from a train as it was stopped at the station for water. The robbers confronted the fireman and ordered him to move the engine and car two miles down the track. Much to their irritation, the would-be holdup men had mistakenly unhitched the express car. Realizing they had botched the robbery, the outlaws ordered the fireman to move the locomotive back toward Bellemont and fled into the nearby mountains with no loot.

Collectively, these incidents reveal why some people viewed train robbery as a crime worthy of the death penalty. In each case, the bandits had employed firearms to intimidate railroad employees; during three of the robberies, shots were fired to compel surrender of the train. In the August 10, 1887, in a heist outside of Tucson, the holdup men shot directly into the locomotive cab; miraculously, neither of the occupants was injured, although news reports indicated that a bullet had passed right under the nose of the fireman, burning his lips and cutting off a portion of his moustache. Most important though was their attempts to derail the trains placing both the employees and passengers at risk.

In May, 1888, an incident occurred near the Mexican station of Aqua Zarca, about twelve miles south of Nogales, Arizona, in Sinaloa County, Mexico, that revealed the deadliness of train robberies. In this case, six bandits killed two men and seriously wounded two others; all for a reported haul of $130. Reports from around the country describing the ease in which the robbers could stop a train, relieve it of its valuables, and escape authorities, added to local concerns over railroad heists. The Arizona Weekly Journal-Miner newspaper, published in Prescott, Arizona pointing out the general actions taken by train robbers,

> *"One or two masked men stopped a train laden with passengers and railway hands, then rifled through their pockets, which had a tinge of the ludicrous since there was no money in the mail car and the train did not even have a Wells Fargo car."*

Although in most cases passengers and employees were not molested, enough train wrecks ended in injury or death to generate support for passing the law that made making train robbery a capital crime.

Consequently, railroad interests frequently lobbied the United States Congress to make robbery of any sort a federal crime. Their efforts finally succeeded with the enactment of the 1902 Train Robbery Act. Although the law fell short of making train robbery a capital offense, it did make it a federal crime to board a train with the intent of committing a robbery or murder.

Even prior to passage of the 1902 federal law, train robbery was a difficult undertaking. After any railroad heist, local sheriffs and their deputies were soon on the trail of the perpetrators. Train robbing almost always involved a violation of postal laws, bandits often felt heat from federal authorities as well as county officers and then they had to deal with railroad detectives. U.S. Marshals also pursued train robbers vigorously, but the chronic lack of resources and manpower, particularly in the western United States territories, hampered their efforts. Corporations that were victimized more than made up for the shortcomings of federal authorities supplying their own bounty hunters and lawmen. The Wells Fargo Company hired their own detectives and agents to prevent robberies. The Pinkerton National Detective Agency frequently stepped in to help, in the employment of railroads and express companies, to hunt down bandits.

With the odds thus stacked against them, by the late 1880's bandits were increasingly likely to be killed or captured when attempting a train robbery. Then by 1893, the Southern Pacific Railroad stated that more than 80% of the criminals who preyed on its trains were apprehended. William Pinkerton, a spokesman of the Pinkerton National Detective Agency, was once quoted as saying that two-thirds of the holdup men were killed before, during, or after a robbery and the survivors were captured or driven out of the country.

Nonetheless, train robberies were frequent enough to convince some state and territorial lawmakers that drastic measures were needed. In February of 1889, Lewis Martin, a newly elected representative to the Arizona Territorial Legislature from Pima county, introduced a sensational bill that would make train robbery a capital offense to go along with the law that was a couple years earlier passed by the New Mexican government.

Martin was born in Massachusetts and moved to California as a youngster and except for a four-year stint working for the United States Navy he spent most of his adult life working for the Wells Fargo Company. Later in his career, he ran the Messenger Service Division of the Southern Pacific Railroad.

At the time of his election to the Arizona Territorial legislature, Martin had been an engineer on passenger and freight trains that ran between Tucson and El Paso, Texas, for eight years. It is safe to assume that his first-hand experience dealing with train robbers and the effects of train robberies made him keenly aware of the dangers posed by such train robberies. The Bill that Martin introduced in the Arizona Legislature was similar to the 1887 New Mexico statute that was instrumental in putting a halt to the train robberies in that territory.

It is unclear how much support Martin's proposal initially received. But a few days after Martin introduced his bill local, syndicated newspapers all over the country, carried the story of a brutal robbery on the Southern Pacific line near Pixley, California. Two masked men boarded a train as it rolled from the station. About two miles out, one of the bandits pointed a shotgun at the engineer and ordered him to stop the locomotive. The holdup men then escorted the fireman and the engineer back to the Wells Fargo express car. The Wells Fargo messenger agent refused to open the door.

While the bandits were planting dynamite under the car, the train's conductor sensed trouble and summoned the help of passengers, especially Ed Bentley, a deputy sheriff from the nearby town of Modesto, California, along with one of the railroad's train detectives, George Gabert, who both just happened to be on that very train. The three men and a brakeman were working their way back to the express car when the robbers spotted them and opened fire, killing Gabert, mortally wounding Ed Bentley and forcing the others to retreat. As soon as the dynamite exploded, the bandits emptied the strong box of $2,500 and escaped on their horses that had been tied to a telegraph pole.

The Arizona legislature passed Martin's bill on February 28, 1889, ironically on the same day the news of Bentley's demise reached the Territorial Capital in Prescott, Arizona. On March 2, 1889, then Territorial Governor Conrad Meyer Zulick signed the bill into law. A few weeks later, the Prescott Arizona Weekly Journal Miner newspaper commented on the large amount of free publicity the territory was receiving. An editorial article published on March 20, 1889, by the New York Herald noted approvingly,

Chapter Three

It is important to present the history of the area surrounding the railroad town of Canyon Diablo. This includes the canyon itself, the railroad train station named for the town, as well as Two Guns, a nearby settlement. This gives context and perspective to the history of the surrounding area as well as pictures of the terrain where the famous train robbery and three-week pursuit took place.

The history of the area around Canyon Diablo, Arizona, dates back to the Dawn of Man. The first Native Americans who settled the area were the Anasazi and Mogollon Culture. They are also referred to as Pueblo people, because they lived in settlements that looked like our current apartment complexes on the land and in the high cliffs villages that were predominant in the Southwest. Historians believe these people migrated up from South and Central America, somewhere between 2,000 to 5,000 years B.C. But the greatest density of these inhabitants was between 1050 and 1600 A.D. With the maximum Native American population from 1050 to 1300 A.D, when the land on the Coconino Plateau was made fertile by the disintegration of the volcanic fields from the San Francisco Peaks that lay thirty miles west.

Long before Man lived in this area, some 22,000 years ago according to scientists, a giant nickel-iron meteor weighing several million tons and travelling at a speed of 133,000 miles per hour, plunged into the earth creating a huge crater just east of Canyon Diablo destroying all life for a one-hundred-mile radius. The meteor is estimated to have been about 81 feet in diameter. The crater left after impact was and still is nearly a mile in diameter and 600 feet deep. Artifacts found in the crater indicate that an unknown ancient culture tried to live within the rim of the crater, but found it to be unsuitable.

Meteor Crater *(as it is known today)* wasn't considered to have been caused by a meteorite until 1886, when Navajo sheepherders found pieces of meteorites near Canyon Diablo. In 1891, a leading geologist, G. K. Gilbert, declared that the crater had not been made by a meteor. It wasn't until 1903 when Dr. Daniel Barringer, a mining engineer, convinced that a large metallic meteor had created the crater, began drilling at the site, but he was unsuccessful in mining any real mineral ore. His project to locate the main mass of the meteorite was abandoned in 1929 after drilling to a depth of nearly 1400 feet on the southeastern slope of the crater. His research revealed that about 80% of the meteorite had been vaporized on impact and that only about 10% of it still lies beneath the south rim.

On the previous page is a railroad postcard of Meteor Crater a copy of which the author owns.

The first known Europeans to see Canyon Diablo and Meteor Crater were the Spaniards from part of Coronado's expedition into New Mexico in 1540-1542. They were led by Captain Don Garcia E. Cardenas, who had been sent by Francisco Vazquez de Coronado to find the Grand Canyon of the Colorado River, and they crossed Canyon Diablo during their expedition.

Over the next 300 years, many explorers, settlers, traders and treasure seekers, trying to establish a direct route to the beautiful San Francisco Peaks on the western horizon and from there to the Pacific Ocean, were confronted with the 300-foot chasm of Canyon Diablo and were forced to make a detour of some 25 miles either north or south in order to find a crossing place of the canyon with the Little Colorado River lying below at the bottom of the long, steep walled canyon. In 1853, Captain Amiel W. Whipple, during his historic thirty-fifth parallel survey, working for Secretary of War Jefferson Davis, in the cabinet of President Franklin Pierce, reached the edge of the deep gorge and dubbed it Canyon Diablo *(Devil's Canyon)*. Captain Whipple wrote in his journal the following,

> *"We were all surprised to find at our feet, in magnesium limestone, a chasm probably two hundred fifty feet in depth, the sides precipitous, and about three hundred yards across the top. A thread-like rill of water could be seen below, but descent was impossible. A railroad bridge could be built, as the banks of*

the canyon would provide plenty of stone and a solid foundation for it."

Spanish records indicate that Spanish explorers were passing through continuously from New Mexico through the area starting around 1750. The first Americans to see the canyon were mountain men and fur traders, first arriving in 1825. They trapped for beaver along the Little Colorado River, which until the late 1880's contained a heavy growth of cottonwood trees and thick patches of willows that extended out into the mud flats.

After the American occupation of the southwest, the regular route from the east in a direct line to the San Francisco Peaks on the horizon led traders and travelers right to the edge of the rim of the chasm known as Canyon Diablo. From the Indians, the travelers learned access points and routes that allowed them to get down into the long steep walls of the canyon, to the water that lay at the bottom. They were able to cross the river a few miles up or down the river from the points the Indians showed them and get back up the steep walls on the other side. All along the walls were hundreds of names carved into the rocks.

In 1854, only one year after Captain Whipple had been through the country and made his survey, Felix Aubrey, a Santa Fe trader, laid out the first wagon route traveling with sixty men, eastward along the existing trail, across the northern portion of the Arizona Territory from San Jose, California to Santa Fe, New Mexico. When the party reached the west rim of Canyon Diablo, he was baffled as to how he could cross the steep canyon until Indians told him he could detour downstream. He then proceeded north along the rim to the regular crossing. While at Canyon Diablo, he met a large number of Indians, who traded him $1,500 in gold nuggets for some old clothing and blankets, but they wouldn't disclose the source of the gold. After finally reaching Santa Fe, New Mexico, he was killed in a duel in August of 1854. His route was known after that as the California-Santa Fe Trail.

A recent photo of Canyon Diablo, taken by Jeff Dunn and used with his permission

The next major survey of the 35th Parallel was the famous Beale Camel Project in 1857. The Secretary of War, Jefferson Davis was largely responsible for this seemingly bizarre endeavor of using camels to pack supplies and equipment from Fort Defiance, Arizona, to California's eastern frontier. Seventy-nine camels, imported from the Middle East through Texas seaports were led by

Arab, Greek, and Turkish camel drivers and commanded by the colorful Ned Beale, later to become well known as the one who carried the news of the California gold strike to President Milliard Fillmore.

On September 8, 1857, Beale's expedition reached the rim of Canyon Diablo. His guide had warned him that he could not cross this chasm so far south of the Little Colorado River, but he had to find out for himself. Going north to the old trail he found a crossing point. At this time the trail was designated as the Beale road. But, due to the high cost of the Civil War the United States government scrapped the Camel Project.

The Civil War, had ended what had been and would have been a successful experiment using camels, that were able to carry an average 800 pounds each of freight and able survive on the desert vegetation. Unlike mules that had to eat hay that also had to be transported with the caravan, along with carrying a maximum of 250 pounds of freight. Plans for a railroad to the west were put on hold until the 1880's, and the camels were sold or sent into the wild or sent to auction. Beale's camel trail eventually became part of Route 66 and these days it is now Interstate 40.

Chapter Four

In this chapter the author will discuss the history of the Wolf Trading Post and Crossing, a vital canyon crossing near the towns of Canyon Diablo, Two Guns, and other towns located in northeastern part of Yavapai County, and used by the Indians for centuries to cross this long, steep and deep gorge.

The history behind Wolf Trading Post is very significant as it later relates to the Canyon Diablo Train Robbery. It is a saga of Hermann Wolf, who was from Germany; his relatives were high in the military ranks and were titled figures of old Prussia. There has always persisted the tale he fled Germany following a duel on the field of honor. There is nothing to explain the reason he came to America. He was a very big man, well over six feet tall. He had a large frame and had gray hair as a young man. He rode with Kit Carson's Mountain Men in the day when beaver trapping was a good way to make a living until about 1883, when beaver pelts became an out of date item of the past.

In 1838, Wolf met William Bents on the Arkansas River, who said Hermann Wolf was a practical, blue eyed German. Bents and Wolf partnered with two other of Kit Carson's men, W. E. "Billy" Mitchell, who hailed from Ohio, and Fred Smith, who came from Texas. The four men roved far and wide over the southwest looking with disappointment at the havoc wrought by the disappearance of both beaver and the beaver trade. One year they hit it lucky on the Gila River. With money in his pocket Wolf took off up along the

Little Colorado River after the U.S. Army took the southwest from Mexico in 1846.

They found a crossing in the middle of the long and deep Diablo Canyon, lined with willows and cottonwood trees and plenty of beaver. Wolf trapped west along the stream, went down into the Grand Canyon, up the big Colorado, and east in the spring of 1848. Near what is now the Town of Holbrook, Apaches jumped him early one morning. They robbed him of every fur he packed on two Missouri mules.

Wolf escaped and went on to Santa Fe and Taos, New Mexico. He also worked in the valley of the Green River in Utah in 1857. He once again went to Taos in the winter of 1859, and from there he traveled down into southern Arizona. The outbreak of the Civil War found him once more in Taos. He is said to have travelled over the long trail toward Saint Louis, Missouri, but from there on for the next five years there is nothing concerning him except an unconfirmed story that he served with neither the North or the South armies in the Civil War.

After the Civil war ended, Wolf traveled once more to Taos and Santa Fe, New Mexico. In the fall of 1866, he followed the Rio Puerco River to the west to its junction with the Little Colorado River. Wolf then wandered easterly along the river trails until January of 1867. He then turned west and traveled until he ran into the Big Colorado River. Later that spring he gathered furs of various local animals, and by that fall he was back laying his plans for the winter

Bands of Navajos were living north of the river. The Apache and the Piute roved along the southern border of the Navajo country, along the Little Colorado River seeking scalps and spoils. Wolf was able to elude them or possibly went among them without molestation except in the spring of 1868. Somewhere near Tucker Flat, which is located just west of Winslow on the Little Colorado River, he was jumped by a band of White Mountain Apache Indians.

Wolf did not run. He turned on the Apaches and in an hour killed four and fought his way through to the north side of the river with his pack animals, furs and supplies intact. By the time summer arrived Wolf reappeared on the Little Colorado River again, but now he was accompanied by three Mexicans driving nearly a score of mules and horses that Wolf planned to use to trade for items he needed with the Indians and other trappers. Moving his outfit to a spot twelve miles below the Hopi ford, he halted on a high ridge along the top of Diablo Canyon that overlooked the river. There is where he saw the place a couple miles ahead where he and his friends had trapped earlier that had the huge grove of cottonwood trees and willows, so they headed on down to the valley.

When they arrived they unpacked and set to work snaking cottonwood logs and slender willows to the site. They dug and tore a trench into almost solid sandstone in order to erect a one-room stockade approximately twenty feet wide and forty feet long. One heavy door was made. No openings were left for windows, only slatted holes through which a rifle muzzle could be poked. The floor was rock on which the structure stood. When finished it was christened Wolf Trading Post.

Wolf delayed sending the Mexicans home. He knew the Navajos were moving just north of him on the plateau above the canyon, and several raiding parties of Apaches were raiding the plateau on the south side of the canyon where they were located. However, the closest raiding party was several miles south of him near what was a small trading post called Two Guns.

One night a large party of Navajos crossed the river below the trading post. Wolf saw them with his field glasses. They did not stop but waved as they rode south toward Two Guns. The armed riders were on a mission as the Navajos were known for farming and ranching. Wolf figured they were after raiding Apaches.

Two days later the Navajo war party rode leisurely back, this time they stopped at Wolf's Trading Post. They had many horses and loot they had taken in a battle with the Apache war party that had been hiding out in a cave in Diablo Canyon near Two Guns. The chief had a little cash they obtained from trading with Mormons in southern Utah. Before leaving Wolf's Trading Post they bought and traded some of the loot they had taken from the Apaches for tobacco, cloth, coffee and a little sugar. They were just learning how to use coffee.

Word of Wolf's Trading Post traveled up and down the land among the Indians. Very soon a few more Indians began slipping into the post to trade goods. They generally arrived after dark and were on their way before daylight so they could avoid their enemies. Traders started to arrive on a regular basis, the Hopi Indians from the north, Piute Indians from the Willow Springs area to the southwest and some Apaches from the Tonto Basin country, all became regular customers. It was more business than Wolf ever dreamed. It soon became necessary to either close up his small store or else get in more goods to trade.

Not desiring to leave the post, Wolf sent his three Mexican workers east accompanied by a dozen stalwart Navajos with their light ponies. As protection for them he sent along a letter to the Navajo Agent at Ojo Del Osa *(Old Fort Wingate, New Mexico)*. They departed marveling at this man who would stay alone on the river, and believed in their own minds that upon their return they would find only his bones in ashes and the stockade burned.

However, one month later when they returned the place still stood. Wolf was alive and well. A band of Navajos had come out of the Painted Desert to live across the river from him. Hosteen Redshirt was their leader and district chief.

Over the next ten years, Wolf had many skirmishes with renegade Apache and Piute Indians. It was lucky for Wolf that Navajo Chief Redshirt kept his camp across the river from the Trading Post. Redshirt and his braves came to the rescue of Wolf on many occasions. Although Wolf fought gallantly, he was happy to have the Navajo village right across the river from the trading post.

Business was booming and Wolf had regular deliveries from Santa Fe of dry goods, cloths, guns, ammo and other supplies that he could trade with Indians and other settlers as they passed by his trading post on their way to or from the south or the north. Instead of actually going out and getting his own furs, Wolf taught the Navajos to do the work for him, then he traded with them to supply them the dry goods, food and clothing they needed to survive and he did this at a substantial profit although the Navajos were very happy with the arrangements.

In the summer of 1874, a party of Mormon immigrants crossed Lees Ferry and moved down the basin of the Little Colorado River from the site of present day Cameron, Arizona, to Wolf Trading Post. They camped a few days on the north side of the river from the trading post while they built a dug-way over the river. The ford was thereafter, called Wolf Crossing.

By the late 1870's the trail to Wolf Trading Post and Wolf Crossing became well-traveled, as it was one of the only ways to get through Diablo Canyon. Mormon wagon trains rolled past in increasing numbers. By this time there were several trails that had been developed in the area and Wolf Trading Post became a stop for many immigrants, Indians, miners and ranchers, on their travels from the north and the south along with outlaws that would also pass by the post.

The Apaches made one more try to take the Post, in October of 1870. They got no closer than Canyon Diablo near Two Guns, where they turned back upon discovering the Navajos rallying to meet them. In Sunset Pass they met up with the Fifth U.S. Cavalry and a sharp fight ensued.

Survey crews for the A & P Railroad made their way from the east between Wolf Trading Post and Two Guns on the California Trail *(Interstate 40)*. The year 1875 saw an increase of traffic along the California Trail. Miners, immigrants, cattle and sheep ranchers invaded the fertile areas in the river basin. Mormon settlers were flocking southward, from there to many parts of Arizona. Not many miles on up the river from Wolf Trading Post lay Brigham City, Utah, that was first called Ballenger and was founded in 1876.

Wolf's Trading Post was robbed five times during the year 1880. Each gang numbered from two to six members. They took food and clothing for the most part, and money only twice. Being vulnerable to robberies, Wolf decided to make a change. A few hundred feet to the east on somewhat higher ground he erected a building made of stone. In the shape of a square the original small post containing a front room was used as the store and a long back room for cooking and sleeping. It was two years later that Wolf added a larger building behind the store which had small cubby-hole rooms but the new building was a great fortress.

In November, 1881, the tracks of the A & P Railroad were built to the East Edge of Canyon Diablo, four miles south of Wolf Trading Post. At the edge of the canyon construction was halted until the steep canyon sides could be bridged. A small boom town sprang into existence. Dance pavilions, bordellos, bars, gambling dens, restaurants and small stores came into being until the railroad would finally reach Flagstaff in 1883, which then briefly also became a boom and railroad town.

With the completion of the A & P Railroad tracks over Canyon Diablo in late 1882, the railroad saved Wolf from the expense of hiring teamsters to bring trade goods from Santa Fe and made it easier and more cost effective to get his trade goods from the rail at Canyon Diablo Station. Wolf was well along in years and the business no longer meant a great deal to him. He communicated with relatives in Germany, and from across the seas he had shipped at frequent intervals barrels of bottled Rhine wine.

With the coming of the railroad, civilization broke the solitude at Wolf Trading Past. It also took away the travelers of the main immigrant trails, which was some compensation. Wolf started hiring clerks to work his store. Most of his time, and especially after 1890, he spent most of his time resting in a big chair. Indian products filled the stockade, now primarily used as a warehouse. A legend grew up about the old man, and rumors were that he kept an untold wealth hidden about the post. He seldom left it, and when he did, it was to bring in a wagon load of merchandise from the nearby train station at Canyon Diablo. Cowboys continually had difficulties moving their herds through Wolf Crossing, as they alleged the ranchers were encroaching on their land. Wolf on many occasions averted warfare.

In January of 1899, Wolf corresponded with his brother, Francis Wolf, a retired major-general of the German Army. Embarking on a world tour, Francis Wolf wrote his brother that he would leave his ship in San Francisco, California, and pay him a visit at his lonely post. The last week of August, Hermann Wolf went alone in his freight wagon to Flagstaff to await his brother's arrival. He took sick in Flagstaff and on the second day of September, as his brother's trip was delayed, Wolf set out on the return trip to the post, sending instructions to his brother to come to the post with a local teamster when he arrived at Flagstaff. Wolf arrived back at the post in a very weakened and sick condition, but he would not let his helper send for a doctor. Finally, when Wolf became unconscious a messenger was sent to nearby Canyon Diablo to send a telegraph to Flagstaff for a physician to come to his aid.

In the meantime, Major-General Wolf had arrived in Flagstaff when the message reached a local doctor named Miller. Major-General Wolf accompanied the doctor back to Wolf Trading Post. They took the first train east out of Flagstaff to Canyon Diablo. When they arrived at the Trading Post late on the evening on September 4, 1899, they found that Hermann Wolf had passed on at around nine o'clock the previous evening.

While there, Major-General Wolf, handled the funeral arrangements and sold Wolf Trading Post to George McAdams and George Babbitt, from the administrator of the estate, J. H. Lind. Wolf Trading Post continued to operate until 1903 with McAdams as resident partner.

Immediately after Wolf's death all the rumors of his buried wealth arose anew. Seekers after the hoard dug up the country around the old post. They even dug the mud filled cracks in the cliff face of the river canyon. There seems little doubt that Wolf did have a large sum of money hidden somewhere in or around the immediate vicinity of the store because he hardly ever left the place to spend his money.

After a few months of treasure seekers flocking to Wolf Trading Post, fights and shootings became a daily event. The Navajos feared for their lives and they decided it was time to attack these people who were threatening their lives. After several fights between the Navajos and the treasure seekers, including the deaths of several Indians and a few of the invading whites, Wolf Trading Post was closed down for good by the new owners. A part of Arizona History ended when Wolf Trading Post closed.

What remains of Wolf Trading Post. This photo was taken by the author

Chapter Five

The unusual town of Two Guns is very near the half-way mark between Flagstaff and Winslow on the south side of Interstate Highway 40. The exit is well marked and what remains of the ghost town is less than a mile from the highway and can easily be seen from Interstate 40.

The surrounding area of the Coconino plateaus' rolling ranges, ringed by distant mountains, has played an important role in western history since the coming of the dawn of man. The first aboriginal inhabitants were followed by the Basket Makers, and then the Pueblo I and Pueblo II periods, as shown by their typical cliff dwelling ruins in Canyon Diablo and its tributaries.

Pottery pieces recovered at Two Guns have been carbon dated by archeologists placing the pottery there between 1050 and 1600 A. D. From 1050 to 1300 A.D. saw the greatest Indian population that the region has ever had. This was due to fertile farming land on the plateau created by disintegration of the volcanic fields of lava and the ashes that once spewed out of the San Francisco Mountains skyline north and west of Two Guns.

The same fiery meteor already discussed earlier in this book, that hit the area some 22,000 years ago, plunged to the earth east of Two Guns. Some scientists believe that the mass that weighted several million tons, and may have been part of a planet that once existed in orbit between Mars and Jupiter in our own solar system. It is thought by scientists that the planet was destroyed by a great cosmic explosion. Upon striking the earth, the meteor created a vast hole in the earth's surface known today as the Barringer or the Meteor Crater.

Oral historians from the local Navajo tribe have revealed that a cave in Canyon Diablo under what remains of Two Guns was used by Apache raiding parties to hide from their Navajo enemies. And was also used to launch attacks on unsuspecting Navajo villages that lay just twenty miles north of the cave on the north side of Canyon Diablo, a few miles north of the Little Colorado River at Wolf's Crossing.

The Apache and Navajo tribes often had battles in and around Canyon Diablo near Wolf's Crossing, even after the arrival of the white settlers in the southwest. From the earliest years of settling in what is now Arizona, the Navajos used a well-traveled trail from the north passing along the east side of Canyon Diablo just past Two Guns. It went through Chavez Pass and over the Mogollon Rim into central Arizona.

The Hopi Indians talk about the great canyon and river far to the west. Coronado dispatched an explorer by the name of Cardenas to search for it. He was led by Hopi guides. The rather small party came down from the mesa villages to the Little Colorado River, then crossed the Little Colorado River, between Winslow and Leupp at a location that was only known by the Hopi guides.

The party turned northwest in order to pass above the San Francisco Peaks on the blue skyline. Following downstream, they crossed Canyon Diablo near where it enters the river on the flatland. The party was led by Captain Juan Melgosa and arrived at the edge of Grand Canyon but failed in an attempt to descend into the mighty gorge down to the Colorado River. The upper end of the Painted Desert, from Leupp to north of Cameron was named after the Spanish explorer, the Melgosa Desert.

The Spanish explorers of the mid 1500's named the canyon from the fact that it was almost impossible to get down the sheer walls to the riverbed itself except at a few places only known to the Navajo and Hopi Indians. Thus it was named Canyon Diablo, or in English the Devil's Canyon.

It is uncertain whether the Melgosa exploring party or a later party lead by Antonio de Espejo may also have named the canyon in 1582. That autumn Espejo set out from the village of Zuni accompanied by nine men on a silver prospecting expedition.

Proceeding west to the Hopi villages they visited other villages including Wupatki, Shungopovi, Mishongovi, Oraibi and Awatobi. From the latter pueblo, not on a mesa, Espejo took four of his men and Hopi guides southward, exploring new country.

After crossing the Little Colorado River, they came in against Canyon Diablo off the Navajo Trail somewhere near Two Guns. With the vertical walls preventing a crossing, they continued on up the east side. Passing somewhere south of the now location of Kinnikinick Lake and they reached

Stoneman Lake, proceeding from there south into the Verde Valley of central Arizona.

The Pueblo Indians of New Mexico, including the Hopi of Arizona, rebelled and drove out their Spanish conquerors in 1680. Twelve years later Don Diego De Vargas came with another expedition north from Mexico. In New Mexico he finally conquered the rebellious Indians. After accomplishing this task, Don Diego De Vargas sent other exploration parties to the west and south from the Hopi villages, but the other parties only made a few minor discoveries.

It was during this period that the extensive legend of the *"Lost Gold Mines of the Padres"* originated. Explorers are still seeking these legendary and fabulous mines. From translated ancient Spanish documents, they could be anywhere from Two Guns west to the Colorado River or north to Utah's Blue Mountains.

There were several reports of the mines resulting in many unauthorized expeditions of wealth seekers venturing west from New Mexico. Although there have been no authentic records, we know that most of them crossed Canyon Diablo while searching for these mines. At that point they were forced downstream a few miles to where precipitous walls fell away *(Wolf Crossing)*. Those without strict official permission to search for gold and silver did not leave journals behind detailing what they found.

The recorded history of a Spanish exploration party in 1769 is more definite. This record was found by archeologist Melvin McCormick. It was written in stone with an inscription and a cross in a huge rock along the Little Colorado River.

This party was composed of several Roman Catholic Franciscan padres and Spanish soldiers, but was an ill-fated exploration party from the start. The Franciscans padres mined and collected a huge store of silver bars somewhere in central Arizona, and then they set out to transport the treasure by mule train to their church headquarters in Santa Fe. In 1767 the Spanish crown laid claim to all gold and silver found in the New World. So they had to turn over their treasure, and then they were ordered to leave their New Mexico missions.

Coming up over the Mogollon Rim on the Navajo Trail, the train was attacked by Apaches. Constant hit and run assaults by the Apache raiding parties forced the exploration party west and north. They arrived in Canyon Diablo somewhere near Two Guns. Standing off the Indians, the Spaniards followed the river downstream to a point where they could cross.

Spanish documents and maps were discovered in 1902. The explorers were constantly compelled along their journey to dispose of some of the weight overburdening their pack mules. The mules that packed the silver were pushed to the point of death. The mule train traveled part way along the side of Padre Canyon, which was apparently named after the Fathers. Finally, when they reached the Little Colorado River, fatalities from Indian attacks cut them down and all but ten of the Spaniards perished. As a final resort many mule loads of silver bars were cached on the site of an abandoned Indian village.

The survivors of the expedition split into two parties, with five of them making an attempt to escape west into California, and the other five headed east toward New Mexico. From Spanish records only the latter group made it through to their destination. For it was in the musty archives of the Old San Miguel Mission in Santa Fe, New Mexico, that the above-mentioned documents were found.

The map locating the buried silver brought many treasure hunters into the area. On one side of Padre Canyon, 17th century Spanish armor was recovered in 1919. But only one silver bar that was approximately four inches square by about twenty-three inches long and weighing 64 pounds, was found by a sheepherder. This discovery was made west of Two Guns in Bonito Park, and is believed was lost from a pack mule before the rest of the bars were hidden.

It is certain the Spaniards from New Mexico were continually passing through the Two Guns vicinity after 1750. However, no known Americans showed up until 1825 to 1830. As previously mentioned these explorers were there to trap beaver and not to look for the silver bars. The Little Colorado River, until the late 1880's, contained a heavy growth of willows and cottonwood timber along its sides which overflowed on to the mud flats. Trappers took beaver along the river and along the streams in the connecting side canyons. After the end of the California Gold Rush from 1849 to 1852, gold miners arrived in the area.

What remains of the Town Two Guns. This picture was taken by Rob Rupp of smugmug.com; used with his permission.

Russell Crowe purchases Ghost Town "Two Guns" in Arizona
By Frank DiAmmato, April 9, 2011

"How would you like to own your own Ghost Town? Got 3 Million dollars to spend?

Russell Crowe has been trying to start production on the film West World for over 12 years now. Russell loves westerns and rumor has it that this film is now on the front burner with producer Jerry Weintraub at the helm. But the original film released in 1973 was written by Michael Crichton.

The Father of the Techno Thriller; Michael owns the rights to the film, and also wants to produce West World Part 2 in 2013.

Russell's solution, simply change the name, now called 'Two Guns'; the film is about two guests at a high-tech amusement park who go on a Wild West adventure. The park is peopled by robots and is designed to provide a 100% life like experience simulating Roman times, cowboy times, and medieval times. When the park's central computer breaks down, the robots start to run amok and our two guests find themselves stalked by a robot gunslinger.

Russell was originally planning to film the movie in Sydney, Australia, so he could stay close to home, however when a friend told him about a Ghost Town that was for sale and on the market in Arizona, Russell decided to have a look himself.

Two Guns is a real ghost town located in Arizona close to Interstate 40. The original owner has been trying to sell it for several years, with a price tag of 3 million, no electric, broken gas pumps, and empty zoo cages and dilapidating ruins, it was not the ideal investment.

However, when both producers, Jerry Weintraub and Crowe, looked at the property, it would also include a portion of some other property know as Canyon Diablo. Canyon Diablo is known as "The worst trail town in Arizona-perhaps the entire West"..."the toughest Hellhole in the West"... and "the West's deadliest town." Between 1880 and 1882, there were more killings as a result of gunfights, robberies, and murders took place there than in Tombstone, Dodge City, and Abilene, Kansas combined.

If Tombstone was noted for 'having a man for breakfast every morning,' then it could be said that Canyon Diablo 'had a man for breakfast, lunch, and supper every day.' The history of Two Guns and Canyon Diablo was just what the film; now called Two Guns needed, some realistic, futuristic and historic embellishments to be included into the story's theme.

For now, Two Guns is closed with a sign on the gate No Trespassers, but in the near future *this Ghost Town will turn into a nightmare of tractor trailers and production crews. Maybe when Crowe is done he will convert it into his living space, Crowe's Hellhole in the West."*

Chapter Six

Contrary to Hollywood movies, most of the Apache were farmers, but like all cultures there is always a bad element, and that element seems to get all of the publicity. Two desert dwelling tribes, the Chiracahua in Southeastern Arizona and the Warm Springs Apache that lived in Southwestern New Mexico held on to the old ways, which was to raid enemy tribes to obtain their food, clothing, pottery, blankets and slaves, killing any brave that stood in their way. These spoils were then used by the tribes or were used to trade for food and other items that they needed to support their lifestyles.

The Apache and Navajo cultures may have descended from the Athabasca, originally plains cultures that followed game, mostly buffalo, transporting their homes along with them when they were on the move. When the buffalo numbers started to dwindle, both of these cultures relocated to the Arizona territory. The Apache relocated in the desert country of Arizona and New Mexico and the Navajo moved on to the Mogollon Plateau. Historians say the move occurred in 1500 A.D.

The Apache easily adapted to the hot, dry deserts of the Southwest from carrying their teepee's from place to place, to designing and building dwellings called wickiups. Wickiups were constructed from the readily available desert willow tree limbs and other brush. After the basic framing was completed, the home was covered with animal hides. The dwellings kept the Apache warm in the winter and cool in the summer.

**A picture of an Apache Wickiup found in
our National Archives, circa 1910**

The Navajo, a bitter enemy of the Apache, and also the Athabasca as mentioned above, relocated to the Mogollon Plateau north of the San Francisco Mountain range. They too adapted to their new surroundings by building hogans. These homes were made out of clay and straw. The walls and ceilings of these dwellings were made up to a foot thick. Some hogans were made from thick aspen logs that were readily available in the forests on their land. They kept the culture cool in the summer months and warm in the bitter cold and snowy winter months. The Navajo were and still are enemies of the Hopi, who lived in the middle of their land. The Navajo and Hopi were farmers, raising stock to trade and also as a food source. Neither tribe subscribed to the old ways of the Apache, with no outright wars.

Historians record that in the late 1500's the Apache would send raiding parties traveling from their desert homes in Southeastern Arizona close to 300 miles north, following the San Pedro river trail to the Gila River and then from just north of present day Globe, Arizona, they followed Cherry

Creek north up the Mogollon Rim trail to Canyon Diablo. They traveled the length of the canyon, hiding in caves, in the steep, deep walls of the canyon, following the Little Colorado River trail that lay at the bottom.

A Navajo Hogan, this photo was also found in our National Archives

The raiding party's intention was simple: attack the unsuspecting Navajo villages to obtain pottery, slaves, highly valued woolen saddle blankets, pottery, livestock and slaves. Then they would trade the spoils of the raids with Mexican citizens, who waited for these spoils with open arms. And of course they killed every male Navajo brave in each village they attacked.

Mountain men and fur trappers were the first white men to see Canyon Diablo in 1838. At that time the Little Colorado River was lined with willow trees and oak trees, as well as thick brush on both sides on both sides of the river. The river was a virtual haven for beaver and they thrived until the mid-1880's when a flash flood with a huge wall of water surged down the canyon, effectively leveling every bush and tree in its path.

At the time these trappers first entered the region though, the river was over populated with beaver and the Indians needed to trade their large supply of beaver pelts, so these mountain men became the forerunners of the trading posts that were later established in the area. They were able to trade with the Navajo trappers who lived on the north side of the river and canyon as well as the Paiute and Apache trappers who lived and trapped on the South side of the river and canyon. At that time these mountain men were trading guns, lead, bullet molds, powder, dye, buffalo robes and cotton with the Indians in exchange for their beaver hides, ponies, blankets and jewelry.

After the American occupation of the southwest, in 1846, the regular route from the east pointed directly to the breath taking San Francisco Peaks visible for upwards of a hundred miles and from there traveling in a direct course east, they collided abruptly with the rim of Canyon Diablo and the Little Colorado River.

The Navajo gave the European explorers directions on how and where water could be found in the canyon during the hot seasons. The Little Colorado River was dry during the summer months, but the Navajo new where water was readily available all year round. One of those places was near the town of Two Guns, located just about two miles downstream from the trail. Water being so vital to every animal, inhabitant or traveler coming from either the east or the west along the trail. But especially with a high need during dry summer seasons when the river was either dry or just had a trickle in it here and there.

Though unknown to early day travelers, the canyon could also be crossed upstream from Two Guns. Long before the 1850 route through the canyon which led downstream a few miles there was a main crossing was regularly used by all travelers. In fact, there are hundreds of names etched in the stone walls nearby.

In trading with the Indians the mountain men received beaver pelts, mules and plain striped handmade woolen blankets known as saddle or wagon blankets, along with beads and pottery. One trader well known to the Navajo for many years was called *"Billikoni Sani," (Old American in the Navajo language).*

Billikoni Sani arrived in the area during the summer of 1852, and he spoke fluent Navajo, indicating that he probably had lived sometime previously among the Navajo people. The amazing magic he performed was mixing raw alcohol that he always carried, with one to three gallons of water, then he added cayenne pepper and chewing tobacco to the brew. This concoction of spirits was called *"Arizona Frontier Whiskey."* Yuck!!

When the Navajo tribal roundup of 1864 began, many Navajo families fled into Canyon Diablo and hid in its' caves to avoid being discovered by U.S. Cavalry Troops. Eight-thousand Navajo were sent to the federal prison at Fort Sumner, New Mexico, for four years. Their livestock and land were taken by the cavalry. They were not allowed back to their land until three years after the war ended in 1865. By the summer of the year 1868 most of the Navajo people were released from Fort Sumner and returned to their homes in the Little Colorado basin.

In 1886 Fred W. Volz established a trading post a few miles north of Two Guns and called it the Canyon Diablo trading post. The trading post was built near the southwestern boundary of the Navajo Reservation, and just a few yards from the A & P Railroad Depot.

Volz remained there until 1910, establishing both a U.S Post Office and a Wells Fargo Stagecoach Station at the trading post. Since the post was painted white, the Navajo referred to it as Kinigai *(White House)*. Fred Volz and his wife were married during these years and had one daughter, Jeanette, who also lived there.

The photo above found in our National Archives the Canyon Diablo Trading Post 1905

However, activity in the area was not at a standstill. Indeed, from 1860 on, sheep and cattle ranchers had located not many miles away, and grazed their animals along Canyon Diablo. The first sheep herder of importance to come to the area was John Clark, who brought 3,000 head of sheep from California to the area for the summer and fall of 1875. The following year William Ashurst, father of one of the first Senators from Arizona, arrived from the east. That same year the Daggs brothers out of Flagstaff, brought more than 10,000 sheep from California.

It was in early November of 1881 when the Atlantic & Pacific Railroad construction gang, consisting for the most part Irish and Chinese immigrants, reached the east edge of Canyon Diablo. They started building the railroad from Fort Smith, Arkansas, across the plains to Albuquerque, New Mexico, and then continuing westward toward Los Angeles, California. They had to halt construction due to the fact that they did not have enough timber to build the bridge over the 255-foot-deep gorge. The timber trestle braces had to be pre-assembled at a plant 250 miles away and then shipped to the canyon edge. It turned out someone misread the plans and the bridge came up fifteen feet short of the other side of the gorge.

This mistake plus other financial difficulties meant that construction was delayed for seven months. By this time, the remarkable Edward Ayers, later to become a chief benefactor of the Field Museum and the Newberry Library in Chicago had assembled a sawmill and taken it to the end of the track. Transporting it by ox-team across the Little Colorado River and on to Flagstaff, he wasted no time in establishing the Ayers Lumber Company provided the lumber for the railroad as it proceeded west.

While waiting for the bridge to be built, the railroad construction shack town of Canyon Diablo grew into a wild place populated by some 2,000 untamed citizens. The yellow-painted depot, the section crew's house, stock pens, a water tank, freight docks and warehouses stood at the western end of the town on railroad property. From there a mile-long row of tin, tar paper and canvas buildings extended eastward along both sides of the one rocky street. The street was aptly called Hell Street. It had fourteen saloons, half of which had wooden fronts and porches. They all had plank wood floors that could absorb beverages that were spilled and kept the patrons from slopping around on mud or dirt floors. Hell Street also sported ten gambling houses, six brothels and two dance pavilions, a grocery store and several eating establishments.

Murder on Hell Street was common and there was a holdup almost every hour. Tales about the exploits of colorful characters at Canyon Diablo, including Billy "The Kid," Keno Harry, Clabberfoot Annie and B. S. Mary.

E. E. Ayer owned the largest lumber mill in the southwest which was located in Flagstaff at the end of the railroad. The lawless conditions stunned him. He had enough political power to demand and receive an escort of soldiers from Fort Defiance, Arizona. With them he got his machinery through. But the presence of troops hardly caused the criminal element to pause in their depredations.

The sawmill owners in Flagstaff along with the town merchants held a town meeting and raised enough money to provide a good salary for a town marshal at Canyon Diablo, in hopes of keeping outlaw element under control. The businessmen's job was simply to interview and hire a town marshal. This proved to be a more difficult job than providing the officer's salary.

The rowdy railroad town had a rapid succession of peace officers. The first marshal was hired after an three o'clock in the afternoon. Sadly, by eight o'clock that same evening he was laid out for burial, shot while in the process of making an arrest.

The second marshal the town council hired lasted a whole two weeks, before the workers ran him out of town on a rail, so to speak, but during his brief tenure as the town marshal, he shot and killed fifteen men in the course of upholding the law and serving arrest warrants in the town of Canyon Diablo. With the town council of businessmen up in arms about so many killings they asked him to leave town.

The third marshal was a sneaky, underhanded character, who carried a shotgun to defend himself in the process of keeping the peace. When he got in a scrape with a bad actor in the process of the arrest, he often peppered innocent bystanders with double O pellets. At the end of three weeks on the job, he received six forty-five caliber lead slugs fired by a disgruntled man between his shoulders ending the marshal's life.

The fourth marshal was a gnarled little man, with piggish black eyes, who made a deal with the outlaw element to help him keep the peace. He actually served for six days, during which there were no crimes committed in the rowdy railroad construction town. On his last day in office, he caught a bandit red-handed in the act of stealing from one of the shops. When confronted, the bandit turned a blazing gun muzzle on the marshal, at point blank range in the dark, and shot him dead with one shot to his chest.

A month passed before the council was able to find a new marshal. Then finally, a rough looking man rode into town. He was an ex-preacher, who hailed from Texas. He was a weathered looking middle aged man with a consumptive cough. He was spotted entering town by the hiring committee, standing in front of Keno Harry's Poker Flat They saw that he wore two low slung guns. Being broke and hungry, he accepted the job that would at least allow him to start eating regularly.

When he was asked to provide his name for the record, he hesitated a bit, obviously deep in thought. Glancing down at the striped ducking pants he wore, he replied smugly saying his name was "Bill Duckin."

Marshal Bill Duckin held the office of Canyon Diablo town marshal for a full thirty days, but he died the day after collecting his first month's salary. During his month long tenure as marshal in the process of serving arrest warrants killed on the average a man a day or thirty men before he bit the dust. He also wounded so many men that the nearest railroad hospital thirty miles east of Canyon Diablo in the town of Winslow refused to accept any more gunshot victims.

Marshal Bill Duckin passed from this world on a Sunday morning the day after payday. Celebrating his recent prosperity and reflecting on the great job he had done in his first month in office, flush with money after putting the squeeze on all the joints in town, he decked himself out in fancy clothes. Imitating other famous town marshals of the day, he provided himself with two, two-button, black bob-tailed coats. The everyday coat had the side pockets cut out that allowed him to get both hands inside his coat to reach his pistols. While wearing his everyday coat, Marshal Duckin could shove both hands down, grasp gun butts and thrust the long barrels between the coats edges; as his special made holsters hung on swivels with the bottoms lopped off. In this tricky way he literally scared bad men to death with his fast accurate draw and shoot skills. The second coat was kept unaltered for Sunday.

On the fatal Sunday morning of his life he strolled along Hell Street wearing his Sunday dress coat; not that he was planning on going to church. He wasn't one to care about the inspirational needs of the 2,000 residents then inhabiting the town. Marshal Duckin was headed for Ching Wong's Beef Stew restaurant for breakfast.

Out of the Colorado Saloon backed a man wearing a black derby hat. Holding a sack of loot in his left hand, he carried a smoking gun in his right. Halting, Marshal Duckin, resting his hands inside the coat pockets, ordered him to surrender. Instead, the bandit opened fire. Too late, Duckin realized he was wearing his Sunday coat and not his everyday coat, as the Sunday coat had no holes in its pockets, so Duckin could not get to his pistols under his dress coat or throw it off in time. Exit Town Marshal Duckin just one day after collecting his first pay.

His successor was Joseph "Fighting Joe" Fowler, who had tamed the booming roar of bad actors in Gallup, New Mexico, when he was the town marshal of that railroad town. A real tough guy without a doubt, he had killed twenty men during his gun-fighting town marshal career.

Fighting Joe lasted just a short two weeks in the office of Canyon Diablo Town Marshal before the outlaws decided to mark him for death. After three narrow scrapes from bushwhacker's without being shot and two other attempts on his life, Fighting Joe skipped town and headed back to New Mexico, from where he came without announcing his sudden departure.

Fighting Joe was only in Silver City, New Mexico no more than a couple of days, when he got out of hand at one of the saloons, and the famous New Mexico county sheriff, by the name of Harvey H. Whitehill, battled Fighting Joe in a standoff hand-to-hand fight in the saloon before Whitehill was able to subdue Fighting Joe, hauling him off to the Silver City Jail. That night an ingrate mob took Fighting Joe from behind his jail cell and decorated a tree with him.

The photo above of a typical railroad town building that was found in our National Archives. This one was in the Union Pacific railroad town, Hell on Wheels in Wyoming.

Town Marshal wasn't the only dangerous job in town. Changing ownership of a saloon or gambling parlor at Canyon Diablo was as simple and expedient as gunning down the owner and then claiming possession. That was how Keno Harry, never known by any other name, obtained his poker flat and that is also how he lost the establishment. He was buried in the town's boot hill cemetery, his grave marker was hand painted and on a simple wooden board stating, *"Keno Harry 1882."* The Canyon Diablo Boot Hill cemetery was located south of the railroad tracks and it had 35 marked graves at one time, but most bodies were buried throughout the town, wherever they fell.

Flagstaff businessmen appealed to the Arizona Territorial Governor Frederick Little for help, requesting the U.S. Army restore order in the town. Sadly, by the time the Army arrived the bridge was completed in June of 1882. It was the highest railroad in the world at that time and built at a cost of $200,000. It was 541 feet long, 255 feet high, using 1,489 cubic yards of concrete.

The first train rolled over the bridge at 3:37 on the afternoon of July 1, 1882. With the bridge construction complete the boomtown of Canyon Diablo died almost overnight. Prior to completion Canyon Diablo had been the railhead for Flagstaff and Prescott, where large loads of train freight were transferred to freight wagons.

Once the bridge was completed, Winslow to the East and Flagstaff to the West became the new freight hubs, effectively ending major commerce at the town of Canyon Diablo, leaving only a railroad station and the trading post. Above is a railroad postcard commemorating the completion of the bridge.

Chapter Seven

In 1884, the Aztec Land and Cattle Company of Boston, began operations in Arizona. Their headquarters were located across the Little Colorado River from the site of Saint Joseph *(now known as Joseph City)*. Aztec Land and Cattle Company became the third largest cattle company in North America. The organization was better known as the Hashknife Outfit, because their brand resembled the old hash-knives used by chuck wagon cooks. The late Zane Grey wrote several novels involving Hashknife Cowboy's.

In 1885 they transferred their corporate headquarters to Holbrook, Arizona. In January of the year 1886 they purchased one million acres of former railroad land from the Atlantic & Pacific Railroad for $0.50 per acre. The ranch claimed a range that stretched some 650 miles from the New Mexico border to just south of Flagstaff, Arizona.

The company then bought the Hashknife Outfit brand and some 33,000 head of cattle and 2,000 horses from the Continental Cattle Company of Texas; at a bargain price because Continental was going broke because of a five-year drought in Texas. When the stock arrived by rail, they were let off the train at stops all across northern Arizona. Along with the cattle and the brand, also came a large number of original Hashknife cowboys.

The small town of Holbrook initially welcomed the money of the cattle company and its associated cowboys until the trouble started and they saw the bad element in action. The buckaroos of Aztec quickly gained an unsavory reputation, hiring some of the worst thieves and killers in the west. The sudden presence of so many bad guys also gave rise to cattle rustling, robbery and gunfights, with much of the cattle thievery perpetuated on Aztec itself.

Above is a photo courtesy of Bill Brown, of one of the Hashknife Cattle Companies ranch and bunkhouses.

Although most of the Hashknife cowboys were good men, there were a number of them who had reputations for being hot-headed and some were outright outlaws. Some of these crooked cowboys were wanted men from crimes committed in Texas and actually were on the run from the law when they conveniently arrived in Arizona on the trains with the cattle. Hashknife cowboys were linked to several train robberies in the Arizona Territory over the years. One of the outlaw cowboys was reported to have stolen a herd of the Outfit's cattle and drove them to Colorado where he sold them. After spending all of his money gambling and visiting the brothels in Denver, he was back on one of the Aztec ranges working cattle again.

Stagecoach and train robberies became a pastime for these Hashknife cowboys and drifters in the area. And, when the cowboys came off the range, with money in their pockets with whiskey and women on their minds, it was time for the Town of Holbrook to hold its' breath. In 1886 alone, there were twenty-six shooting deaths on the streets of Holbrook, which was called home to only about 250 residents at that time.

It was somewhere along this time that the St. Johns Herald reported,

> "The Salvation Army is going to Holbrook, a good field for it operation."

In the meantime, the previously settled small ranchers in the area resented the takeover of the public lands that they had formerly used. One bitter Arizona pioneer wrote,

> "Thousands of longhorns ate all of our grass, along with the riffraff and hell-hounds out of Texas ate small ranchers beef."

The animosity between the two factions soon resulted in even more cattle rustling against the Aztec Land and Cattle Company. The Hashknife cowboys were quick to utilize their guns to keep the small ranchers off their grazing lands.

There was obviously a need for law-enforcement in the Holbrook area and Sheriff Commodore Perry Owens is credited with bringing it to the wild and crusty town in 1887. Within a couple of years, he and his deputy, Frank Wattron, had rid the country of the worst of the outlaw gangs. However, while the town was relatively peaceful, numerous cattle thieves still continued to plague the Aztec Land and Cattle Company Ranch.

In desperation, the Aztec Land and Cattle Company hired Burt Mossman to manage the Hashknife outfit in January of 1898. While living in New Mexico, Mossman had made a name for himself as a successful cattleman and also as a part time town marshal. Mossman immediately declared war on the cattle rustlers and in his first official act, he fired 52 of the 84 men on the Aztec Land and Cattle Company payroll. He then put two men in charge of the remaining cowpunchers and went after the cattle rustlers. By the end of the year, he had sent eleven men to the county jail for cattle rustling. He helped to tame the lawless Town of Holbrook, and the Aztec Land and Cattle Company finally began to show a profit.

It was reported to the local newspaper reporter who overheard Mossman talking to his deputy Frank Wattron as they walked by the Blood Saloon in Holbrook, said,

> "We haven't had a shooting death since last summer. One more would make it 17. Most of the dead men worked for the Hash-Knife Outfit or they were old cowhands that once worked for the Aztec."

Even though the company was finally turning a profit, it was too late to save the Aztec Land and Cattle Company. The next winter was one of the severest to hit northern Arizona. It killed thousands of Hashknife cattle. The following spring, cattle prices dropped dramatically and the company ordered Mossman to liquidate its holdings. In 1901, the ranch was sold to the Babbitt brothers of Flagstaff. Burt Mossman went on to be the first captain of the Arizona Rangers.

Below is a great article that appeared in the Arizona Republic Newspaper on January 27, 2012, written by reporter Ron Dugan is reprinted here. It is a very good summary of the town of Holbrook after Burt Mossman took over running the operation of the Hashknife Cattle Company.

Arizona History: The Hashknife Outfit, from rogues to riders

"It was another Saturday at the OK Bar in Holbrook. Men played poker while a piano player pounded out a tune and a few cowboys sang off-key. Dance-hall girls in gaudy dresses stepped to the music, and glasses clinked at the crowded bar.

A couple of trail bosses began to argue about cattle and sheep on the range, and their words grew heated. Soon the old men stood toe to toe. Their foreman took away their guns, the bosses were too important to the community to be allowed to shoot each other, one of the foremen was quoted. The cowboys crowded around and watched as the two fat men landed punches and drew blood, then rolled on the floor, 'puffing, snorting and blowing with blind rage, Kathryn M. Lathrop writes in 'Hashknives' part of an oral history project funded by the Works Projects Administration from 1937-1940.

The blows came more slowly as the two ran out of strength, yet neither would relent.

The foremen then lifted the men to their feet and shoved them over the bar. Two rounds, they said, courtesy of the trail bosses. Everyone surged to the bar. The foremen bought two more rounds, and the fifth was on the house.

Lathrop's bar fight is a colorful portrayal of a Wild West where nobody gets killed and whiskey flows, but it falls apart upon scrutiny. Lathrop depicts one of the trail bosses as a shady cattleman and rustler who fled Texas, then New Mexico, staying one step ahead of the law and leading a band of rogue cowboy gunslingers known as the Hash-Knife Outfit.

The initial Aztec Land and Cattle Company shareholders didn't know a lot about the cattle business. But livestock was considered a good investment in 1884, the year the company was formed. One board member, Edward Kinsley, had seen Arizona from the window of a train, according to Arizona's Historian Marshall Trimble. 'As he looked out, there was virgin grass out there, the grass was stirrup high and he thought the cattle would flourish because there was enough grass to feed half the nation.'

Aztec Land and Cattle Company bought one million acres of land as previously mentioned for $0.50 an acre from the Atlantic & Pacific Railroad, which had acquired the land as a gift from the U.S. Congress. To promoted investment, the government gave railroads 40 sections of public land for every mile of track they laid. A section is 640 acres. (Totaling 25,600 acres.) On paper, the A & P Railroad became the largest landowner in Arizona history.

By this time, Aztec Land and Cattle Company was in debt but had every confidence that the Arizona investment would turn a big profit. What could go wrong? With so much free-grazing land with tons of bear grass the, cattle herds would surely reproduce, that they were sure their investment would grow in leaps and bounds every year.

There were problems from the start though. One was that the sale of the land to the company was that they owned every-other section of land. The alternating sections were part of the public domain, thusly open to homesteaders willing to make a go of it in the arid West. This pattern of ownership is usually described as a checkerboard. The government set it up this way to reward the railroads for their investment and to encourage settlers to move west.

Much of the land, which was too arid to farm, had not even been surveyed, and few people were willing to chance homesteading. Meantime, the grass was free. Mormon settlers, horse owners, sheepherders and independent cattlemen put their stock out to graze.

The cows didn't know where their land was,' said Trimble. Nobody was sure who owned what, the courts were miles away and everyone had a gun. Chaos ruled the day. Especially in the early days, before they began to use barbed wire, there was no way to regulate that.

> Even if cattlemen had installed barbed wire, it would have been too expensive to fence every section. It was just another example of how screwed up federal land police was west of the 100th meridian, according to writer, Thomas Sheridan. The Hash-Knife cowboys didn't bother figuring out which sections belonged to them. They turned their cattle loose just like everyone else. Small operators got shoved aside. "They were a pretty wild bunch, according to Trimble."

Sheridan went on to write that some Mormon homesteaders were run off their land. The Mormons had already settled in Heber, Show Low and Snowflake when the Hash-Knife cowboys arrived in Arizona. Just how ruthless were the Hash-Knife cowboys? Separating truth from fiction is difficult. Newspapers of the day were notoriously partisan and careless with facts and most court records have been conveniently lost or have mysteriously disappeared.

The Hashknife Outfit may have earned its reputation as a rough and tumble outfit, but they were all not killers and weren't all gunman either. Certainly there was violence in the Arizona Territory. Just about every western town had its period of lawlessness, although it usually ended quickly. There was too much money invested in the West to turn it over to renegade cowboys and drifters. Part of the problem was that the west was settled right after the Civil War, and hard feelings still simmered,

> "There were racial tensions and," Sheridan said, "probably a lot of post-

> traumatic stress, though there were not psychiatrists to diagnose it."

The Railroads allowed transients and outlaws to come and go quickly. Trimble went on to say,

> "You had those guys roaming around, and you mix in alcohol and guns, it is obvious how things got pretty violent."

Aztec had become partners with Eastern investors and Western cattlemen, but it was still perceived as a big outfit owned by wealthy outsiders. The locals figured it wouldn't miss a few cows and stole some from time to time. Even Hash-Knife cowboys stole Aztec cattle. The company tried to solve the problem in the courts, without gunplay, but local juries just turned the accused thieves loose.

As the company struggled with thefts and debt, and as it pleaded for land surveys to determine property lines, a drought overtook the state. By the early 1890's, it was clear that the range was overstocked. Thousands of cattle died. In 1898, Aztec Land and Cattle Company shareholders voted to sell the land, cattle, horses and other property.

> "It hardly ever made money, Sheridan went on to say, and that's one of the reasons it got broken up. Ranching was really volatile business, especially in those early years when there wasn't any kind of regulation. As hard as ranching was, there was no shortage of men and women willing to give it a try.

> *There's a lot of romance about horses and horsemen, you find that all over the world it was more romantic to work cattle on horseback than it was to plow a field behind a mule."*

Aztec Land and Cattle Company sold the Hash-Knife brand and some of its cattle to a local rancher named Jim Wyrick, who was financed by the Northern Arizona pioneer Babbitt family. The Babbitts acquired the brand when Wyrick went broke. Sheridan said,

> *"Like other ranchers, the Babbitts struggled at times,"*

But they remain in the cattle business today and still own the Hash-Knife brand. A line of pure bred horses has been named after it. Sheridan also said,

> *"The Hash-Knife brand name seemed destined for hyperbole, like a flashing through the cattle heavens, while the more tedious Aztec Land and Cattle Company name seemed to fall out of sight."*

But Aztec Land and Cattle Company still exists, more than 100 years later, and operates as a major landholding company. It took a while, but the surveys were completed, and Arizona real estate became more valuable over time. Land surveys and holding companies make poor fodder for Zane Grey novels, however, and so the old stories live on, partly true but embellished over time. A Zane Grey quote,

"The piano is playing, the cowboys are singing, the girls are dancing and the trail bosses are brawling. Its Saturday night, boys, drinks, drinks for everyone."

Chapter Eight

William Owen "Buckey" O'Neill was born in St. Louis, Missouri, on February 2, 1860. William was the oldest of four children. His parents were Captain John Owen O'Neill and Mary McMenamen O'Neill. Both of whom were born in Ireland and migrated to the United States of America when they were young children. While William was a baby, the family moved permanently to Washington, D.C.

Captain John O'Neill served in the Army throughout the Civil War. He organized Company K of the 116th Pennsylvania Volunteers which was the start of the *"Fighting Irish"* brigade. He served with great bravery and received fourteen wounds. In his later life he was usually seen on crutches, or in a small wheeled chair, which he used with great skill that enabled him to go almost anywhere that he went before he was wounded.

Buckey's youth years were spent in Washington, D.C., which was a small city at that time and surrounded by miles of forests, hills and streams. Young Buckey and his pals played, gathered nuts and fruits, fished and hunted squirrels in the nearby forests. O'Neill was given a thorough education under the strict supervision of his father, who had the fine Irish respect for learning and was himself a true scholar. O'Neill graduated from Gonzaga College in Washington D.C., a four-year full credited university, located in D.C where he completed their course, graduating in 1879. After graduating from law school, and a hankering to go west from studying, looking for excitement, Buckey headed for the Town of Tombstone, in the Arizona Territory.

At that time, Tombstone was the new boomtown in the Old West that was created when Ed Schefflin found gold and silver. He was told by an Army Lieutenant stationed in nearby Fort Huachuca, Arizona, if he continued to work his mine in that area with the Apaches on the warpath that he would be buried with his own tombstone. That is how the town received its name. O'Neill settled in Tombstone in 1880, during the same time the Earp brothers were the city policemen and at war with the Clanton-McLaury Cowboy Gang of cattle rustlers and murderers. O'Neill went to work for the Tombstone Epitaph newspaper as a reporter and since it was a pro-Earp newspaper, he frequently talked with and became casual friends of the Earp family.

On October 26, 1881, the war escalated with the Gunfight at the O.K. Corral that took the lives of three of the Cowboy Gang, Frank McLaury, Tom McLaury and Billy Clanton. It is thought by most historians, because of the way the article was written, that it was probably O'Neill that covered the story of the gunfight for the Tombstone Epitaph.

From Tombstone, O'Neill moved to Phoenix where he took a job as a reporter for the Herald Newspaper and made a name for himself as the official reporter writing nationally syndicated articles which brought stories of Arizona to national prominence.

While living in Tombstone, Virgil Earp often spoke about how beautiful it was in Prescott, Arizona. He raved on and on about the four season mild climate. At that time Prescott was the Arizona Territorial Capital.

Prescott served as the Capital of the Arizona Territory from October, 1864, until November 1, 1867. Then the Capital was moved to Tucson by an Act of the 4th Territorial Legislature. The Capital was returned to Prescott in the fall of 1877, by an Act of the 9th Territorial Legislature. Then it was finally moved to Phoenix on February 4, 1889, by the 15th Arizona Territorial Legislature.

So O'Neill decided to move to Prescott in the spring of 1882. Just after he arrived O'Neill took a job as a court reporter and also wrote stories for the Arizona Weekly Journal-Miner newspaper to supplement his income. He was the most noted expert of short-hand in the southwest so he had no problem securing work. While working as a court reporter in Prescott he became interested in mining, stock-raising and general business in the virgin territory of Arizona. He rapidly progressed in his journalistic career and founded his own newspaper, The Hoof and Horn, a paper dedicated to the livestock industry.

O'Neill started to get involved in several different civic organizations when he moved to Prescott. He met Charles Genung, a local cattle rancher, while playing Faro at The Palace Bar. Genung ended up being a lifelong friend of the O'Neill family. They enjoyed many hours of playing poker and gambling at the Faro tables. Charles talked Buckey into joining him as a member of the Prescott Grays, a local Arizona Militia. With Buckey's leadership qualities and grit, he was soon elected captain of the militia in January of 1886. On February 5, 1886 his company of the Prescott Grays was asked to act as guards at a hanging.

The day of the hanging Buckey and his men surrounded the gallows scaffold. Dennis Dilda was hanged. When the trap door sprung and Dilda fell toward the ground snapping his neck, Captain Buckey O'Neill fainted, which caused him severe embarrassment. By this time O' Neill was 29 years old. He stood five feet ten inches tall and weighed around one hundred eighty pounds. He was in excellent physical condition. He had dark brown hair and eyes. He was always seen with a Bull Durham cigar butt hanging from his lips and had a devil-may care attitude. But on this day, after witnessing his first hanging, he told friends that he could not see a man killed without giving him a fighting chance for his life. Buckey later wrote a nationally syndicated story called *"The Horse of the Hash-Knife Brand."* In it, a member of a posse admits to nearly fainting at the proceedings of a hanging of a horse thief.

At this point it is important to show the reader the depth of the personality and writing style of Buckey O'Neill since he brought so much attention to Arizona with his many nationally syndicated newspaper articles.

On the following pages is my favorite article that appeared in the San Francisco Examiner and the Arizona Weekly Journal-Miner newspapers on February 15, 1891 written by Buckey O'Neill:

The Hash-Knife Brand

"It was the Old San Carlos Indian trail, an ancient bridle-path leading from the Valley of the Rio Verde all the way down to the Mexican line. It was a highway so old that the oldest traditions of the Apache tribes gave an inkling of its origin, which was an unusual thing, for life among all savages is such as to be compared with the complex existence of white races that it is rare indeed to find an object or an event connected with them and their history, of which has no a place in their folk lore. The old Indian trails, though, seldom figure in their traditions.

Whether on account of their antiquity or because their existence is such a matter of common everyday life to rob them of romance, no one can say. Yet what tales would be told if each and all who had traveled over these trails of the west were here to tell their stories!

How the Indian first came to travel them; how later the voyageur of France as well as the conquistadors of old Spain; who were followed by the scouts and traders of the west fifty years ago, in turn gave way to the wagon of the emigrant; who in fact was the true pioneer of the west; and, after all of them came the army surveying engineers, running their levels for that personification was the strength and intelligence of the nineteenth century.

The railroad, with all of its ingenuity and science, was the real reason the surveying engineer was able to improve upon those old Indian trails, as pathfinders, were able to be located and improve on the trails the Indians left, and even today there isn't one transcontinental line of a railroad that does not have directions from some aboriginal highway; and for hundreds of miles' parallel with one of these old overland Indian trails, that first lost their identity under such names as Butterfield and Beal.

Over all of them, as over the 'Old San Carlos Trail,' the life which Europe saw within historic days has been repeated, only on a lesser scale. The hordes from which sprang the Goth, the Vandals and Huns, who traveled the bridle paths of the Urals in pushing out from their over-crowded homes in Asia, traveled just such trails. As the trails of the Urals have given way to trans Caspian railways, so have gone the Indian trails of our own west."

The 'San Carlos' is no exception only no railroad engineer has yet availed himself of its strategic worth. The days when war or hunting parties kept all the moisture from the low the grass from obliterating it have passed forever, and only the old-timers seeking a short cut or fugitives fleeing in haste from justice now avail themselves of its rough directness.

Nearly obliterated in places, and in others where it crosses the rugged valleys of the Mogollon Mountains it can be seen, cut deep into the rock by the horse hoofs of the multitudes that have in bygone days passed over it, leaving, like the charioteers of Pompeii, only a mark in the road as a souvenir of their existence.

In one of the places, where the old trail is nearly obliterated, three men are riding. It is long after noon of a spring day. The snow has disappeared a month or more, save on the highest peaks of the mountains, while the warm winds from the south have driven all the moisture from the lowlands, leaving them hard and baked. It is this that makes the work of trailing, or following a person or animal by foot tracks, so difficult.

A month later there would have been dust enough to have held a footprint; a month earlier the winter's snows would have left the ground like a piece of plaster of Paris, as artists prepare it to receive the features of the dead before all is dust.

A broken twig, a bent bunch of grass, a few displaced pebbles, is all that remain to tell whether or not the trail has been recently traveled. Yet the three men seem satisfied with these meager signs and ride on in silence, watching with closer scrutiny the narrow pathway. They are armed with that thoroughness that is as peculiar to the mountaineers of the Rocky Mountains as it is to his brother of the Balkaus of the Himalayas or the Andes.

Occasionally the three men stop like bloodhounds at fault, and which one patiently stands over where is seen the last sign of the traveler they are following, the other two ride off, circling one to the left, one to the right, and seek to recover the sign they lost. When it is found, all three of they start to advance again. For the last few miles the trail has led from the mesas into the mountains until it is impossible to leave.

On all sides of the trail, it is hemmed in the precipitous bluffs, which leads one of the men to remark that they 'couldn't lose it now if we tried.' 'Where do you think you will find the man we are following?' asks the youngest of the three, who is riding in the lead. 'It's hard to tell. He has been riding so fast, though, that he can't travel much farther today, replies the second man.' 'For that matter we haven't even come close to him.' He adds, while he is looking at the jaded horses which the three men are riding Then he speaks, 'right beyond here, though is Fossil Creek, and as that is the last water he or we will strike for twenty miles and we may be able to overtake him.

How does the trail run there?' asks the first speaker. The second man replies, 'it runs right up the creek, so we will need to keep a look out. Shortly after that the lead man advanced the reins of his horse and pointed ahead to where a cloud of almost imperceptible smoke rose in the air not a mile ahead, points and says, 'There he goes.'

At once the three men dismount, leaving one to follow with their horses, as two of the men advance after carefully examining their arms to make sure they were loaded, as they walk forward each pulls his cartridge belt around so that the buckle is behind in order that the greatest number of cartridges may be available if needed, while the revolver is thrown into the position where it can be most readily grasped.

Crawling slowly ahead toward the cloud of dust, taking advantage of every object that would afford concealment, they at last come in sight of a campfire. It was one of those clear spaces found on the banks of all mountain streams. A lit fire built of the smallest and driest pieces of wood was found, in order that the chances of its discovery may be reduced to a minimum, a precautionary piece of woodcraft learned from the Indians, was burning brightly, and over it stands a man roughly clad. Beside him lies in a pile that included a saddle, bridle and blankets, and on top of all within easy reach is a Winchester.

The two men stopped and looked at each other. A glance had satisfied them that their chase has not been a fruitless trek. As the youngest man raises his rifle to his shoulder, his companion places his hand on his arm and whispers: 'Don't shoot, we must take him alive. We will crawl up along the bank there and when we get within twenty feet of him, if he doesn't throw up his hands, when we call out to him, then we can give it to him.

They crawl along the bank until opposite the campfire, when both raised to their feet, with their rifles at their shoulders and called out, 'throw up your hands,' both in almost the same breath. For an instant the man who stands by the fire hesitates, as if debating whether or not to take the desperate chances of resisting. Again the command is repeated and his hands are raised over his head. 'Take off his belt, Jim,' the elder of the two men says, laying down his rifle, the younger man steps forward, carefully standing so as not to be within range of his companion's gun should the man whom he is going to disarm make an attempt to resist, he unbuckles the pistol belt and laying it on the ground examines the man carefully to see if he has any other arms concealed about him. This done the prisoner is ordered to sit down.

He had already done so when the man who has kept guard over the horses comes up. The prisoner looks at his captors curiously, and then he asks in a manner that he strives to make appear almost unconcerned. 'Well, boys, what do you want?' The color has come back to his face, now that the shock of the surprise has worn away. 'What do you think we want?" answers the eldest of the three. "We want to know what you're doing with that hash-knife horse there' he adds, pointing to the big roan that the prisoner has ridden, which has on its flank a brand that is apparently intended to represent a chopping-knife similar to those used in every kitchen for hashing meat.

That horse? The prisoner speaks up and says, 'I bought it from a Mexican at Payson two weeks ago, the prisoner replies.' 'So you did huh. Can you show us a bill of sale for him?' Asks the older man who was speaking says. 'No, the Mexican couldn't write one,' the prisoner answered. The older man speaks, 'Now, what's the use of you lying about it? You know you stole that horse from old man Nash on Tonto Creek, and that you and your gang have been running off our horses for the last six months'

'Me, Bill and Jim have tracked you right up to here, and there is no use of your trying to lie to get out of it.' 'We are going to give you a chance though. If you tell us who has been with you in this business, we will take you back for trial, and if you don't we will try you here and that's about it.

The prisoner remained silent as the color again disappeared from his face. No one knows better than he the penalty of being found with another man's horse in his possession feloniously. He knows, too that the men who sit before him are men who have been rendered desperate by the depredations of he and his companions, and that they will not hesitate to resort to the extreme measures to get free.

He looks at each of the three men as if striving to read their innermost thoughts. As one of them said afterward, 'He looked at them as if he was trying to see if they were bluffing.' 'Well, what are you going to do? Are you going to go back with us and help us clean out the gang, or aren't you?' asks the one who had taken it upon himself the officer who spoke.

I don't know anything about any gang,' said the prisoner with a sullen reply, 'And as for stealing horses, I never did.' 'Oh, no; but that's what you all say,' the inquisitor said as he then turned to his companions exclaims, 'Get the lariat.'

'One of the men at once goes to his saddle, takes a rope from it, and walking back to the group looks he inquiringly at his companions. Although not a word is spoken by either, he seems to be satisfied, and stepping toward the prisoner he throws a loop of the lasso over the prisoner's body, near the waist, and draws it tightly up, thus binding the prisoner's arms close to his side. During this proceeding the prisoner, covered by rifles of the other two men, seems almost inanimate, and attempts no resistance as the rialto is wound tightly around him in such a manner that it is impossible for him to free his hands.

Under the direction of the self-constituted leader another lariat is brought and thrown over a limb of one of the largest of many cottonwood trees that line the bed of fossil creek and the noose was placed around the prisoner's neck, while the man who had been called Bill mounts his horse, and takes several, turns of the other end of the rialto around the horn of the saddle as coolly as if he were lassoing a steer.

'Now, Jack Stanley,' says the eldest of the three men, addressing the prisoner, 'we know you, and if you have anything to say, you had better say it. What's the use of throwing yourself away though on account of the rest of the gang? They wouldn't do it for you. Just tell us their names and how we can reach them, and you can get out of this all right.

There is a tremor in the old man's voice but the prisoner remains silent. He had thought often of his hour as a man thinks of a day that may come. He had never thought it would come so soon or in this shape. Oh, if he had only resisted. If he had only drawn his gun and gone down shooting, instead of standing here to be choked to death like a dog. He cursed aloud in his rage, and called his captors, 'strangers and thugs,' and he begged them to give him some show for his life. 'Well, aren't we?' says one of the three men.

Why don't you tell us whose been helping you? It isn't any use of being so stubborn Jack. The tone was almost coaxing and the prisoner ceased speaking. For an instant it looked as if he might give the names of his comrades, and then the sullen look of defiance came back into his eyes. No, he would not play the traitor. His day was done but he would not drag any of the other 'boys' down with him. They would know he died true and would remember him for it.

Besides, what was the use of living if everybody knew he had weakened to save his own life by sacrificing others? A few minutes bravely borne and all would be over. After all the Indians were right, death was the black horse that came someday into every man's camp, and no matter when that day came a brave man should be booted and spurred ready to ride out on him.

He was a thief and worse, a murderer. He knew that, in his life there had been few things to which he had been loyal; there had been few things, indeed, which he had ever cared for much; but it should never be said that he ever gave the boys away.

How beautiful the world looked, though; how fragrant the budding cottonwood trees smelled. Life had never seemed as sweet as right then and yet he said nothing. 'Well, what are you going to do? Aren't you going to say anything,' asked one of the three." The man spoke;

What is the use? You say I have been stealing horses and I haven't,' was the sullen reply of the captured man. 'You've made up your minds to murder me, and you're going to do it, no matter what I say. When I speak you only say I lie.

The words sound strangely harsh and metallic for they came from a dry mouth with fear-determined as the man is to meet the worse without flinching, he cannot find enough saliva to moisten his lips. 'Do you want to send word to anybody?' asked the youngest of his captors, with a face as white as that of the prisoner. 'Nope! I haven't got anybody to send it too. Only, again I didn't steal the horse.

The old man makes a sign and the next instant the man who was sitting in the saddle on the horse at the other end of the rialto twisted his spurs in his horse and the form of the prisoner is dangling in the air. A few heaves of his chest, two or three spasmodic bending of the body at the knees and hips, a turning in of the arms, a blackening of the face, with turgid protruding eyes and tongue, and then a relaxation of all muscles of his body, and a form that a few minutes before had breathed, hangs straight and limp in the air, turning slowly around like a top that is about to cease spinning.

A few minutes afterward the three men leading a Hashknife branded horse, saddled and bridled, look back from the top of the last *ridge leaving the valley at the body still swaying in the air. Swaying, swaying, swaying as it will sway for days to come, until the vultures and the wind and rope do their work when the neck will give way and a mass of bones will lie scattered around the roots of the tree until the floods of another winter wash them out of sight and then the three men ride back over the Old San Carlos Trail, while the youngest of the party shudders thinking how near he came to disgracing himself by feinting when the body rose into the air."*

In 1884 Captain W. F. R. Schindler was put in charge of nearby Fort Whipple which served as the Arizona Territorial headquarters of Brigadier General George Crook, who had made a name for himself during the battles with the Sioux Indians in North Dakota. He was sent to Arizona Territory to move the Native American population to reservations. Captain Schindler brought his family with him to their new home; including his wife, Rosalie, and their daughter, Pauline, when he arrived at Prescott. Pauline was an elementary school teacher in a Williamson Valley grade school. Buckey first saw Pauline at a medicine show, and he managed to arrange an introduction.

Buckey O'Neill and Pauline Schindler dated for over a year before he finally popped the question. They were married in April of 1886. The day after the honeymoon O'Neill announced his happiness in the newspaper he published called the Hoof and Horn. He described his new bride as *"the right kind of girl,"* as what every man needs to keep his head above water. Pauline gave birth to a son a year after their marriage, but sadly he died shortly after his premature birth. Their thirteen-year marriage seems to have been a happy one, as they were very active in the community. It appears with my research that Pauline may just have been the perfect partner that Buckey wrote about earlier in his newspaper.

Buckey O'Neill was a member of the Republican Party, another reason he was friendly with the Earp family in Tombstone, since they too were Republicans. The Territory of Arizona at that time was primarily Democratic. In any event, after long talks with his close friends in the Prescott Grays and other local politicians, Buckey decided to run for the Office of the Sheriff of Yavapai County in the election of November, 1888. He had the backing of most of the ranchers in the area and that was a big deal at that time.

Just to put this into perspective so you the reader can understand how much money was in the Territory in 1886, it is well documented that Doc Holliday won $40K in five days of gambling at The Palace Bar on Whiskey Row in Prescott. There was no IRS or income taxes at that time. One dollar would have had a buying power today of $137. $40,000 at the time Doc won it would have had a buying power of $5,480,000 according to its buying power today. But one has to take into consideration that Doc Holliday was an alcoholic, gambled on anything anytime and constantly frequented the local brothels and Chinatowns, where he could get his supply of opium and laudanum, which is a mixture of opium and alcohol. He rolled his own cigarettes that were made of tobacco laced with opium. He was dying of tuberculosis and had no reason to save money so he just had a good time. In fact, he was breaking, when he died on November 8, 1887, in Glenwood Springs, Colorado.

Yavapai County, in the Arizona Territory in 1888, was the largest county in the continental United States of America. It stretched from Black Canyon City on the south to the Utah border on the north and the west end started at the Mohave county border and went east to the Navajo Indian Reservation. After a hard fought campaign, William Buckey O'Neill was elected the youngest Sheriff of Yavapai County and the youngest sheriff in United States History. He was sworn into his office on January 15, 1889. Besides his job of keeping the peace in Yavapai County, the sheriff was also the county assessor, responsible for collecting taxes.

An article that appeared in the Arizona Weekly Journal-Miner newspaper the following day stated,

> "On retiring from the office of the sheriff, W.J. Mulvenon presented the newly elected Sheriff Buckey O'Neill with an elegant gold badge, which he had manufactured for Buckey out of high grade Hassayampa Gold he obtained from a mine in Wickenburg, Arizona."

His first order of business upon taking office was to appoint deputies in each area of the county because the county was just too large to keep the peace from his main office in Prescott. With that in mind his first appointment was James Level Black a cattle rancher and part time constable who lived near Flagstaff. Buckey met Black at the Faro tables in the Palace Bar in Prescott. Jim Black's office was in Flagstaff and he was responsible for keeping the peace in the northern and the largest portion of the county.

The next appointment was J. E. Brown who was his Special Deputy in charge of the County Assessor's job. It was Deputy Brown's job to collect back taxes owed the county and to hold auctions to obtain those delinquent taxes. Sheriff Buckey O'Neill finished by appointing as deputies, Jim Roberts, who Buckey had met in Payson and saying,

> "I want the fairest man, fastest, and most accurate shot in the Pleasant Valley War on my side."

Roberts was Buckey's deputy in the eastern section of the county and had his Eastern Yavapai County office in Young, Arizona. He appointed George E. Brown, to handle the south eastern Lower Agua Fria portion of the county. Lewis M. Turner was appointed deputy sheriff to handle the Lower Verde River area. William Denny was appointed his deputy handling the Walnut Creek area, which was the mining area in the Bradshaw Mountains just south of Prescott that ran from Prescott to Crown King. Then his last appointments to be deputy sheriffs were George Ward and P. W. Strahan who were in charge of the Upper Verde area that included the towns of Winslow and Holbrook on the eastern border of Yavapai County.

Buckey also hired Tom Horn as a deputy sheriff, specifically as a tracker. Horn made a name for himself as a top tracker, interpreter and Army scout with General Crook during the Indian Wars. Horn was a government contractor for General Crook and was located at nearby Fort Whipple. Tom Horn also spent a lot of time as a cowboy around the Prescott area, when he was not on maneuvers for the Army. Buckey met Horn at the Faro tables at The Palace Bar.

Tom Horn was an army scout, cowboy and miner in and around Globe when he was not working for the army. He met Al Seiber when he was hired by Sieber to be an interpreter. He was an expert at breaking horses, an amazing roper and he was one of the best trackers and was fluent in the Mexican border language and Apache.

Tom Horn and O'Neill helped organize the first Prescott Rodeo on July 4, 1888. Horn competed against Abram Meadows, also known as "Arizona Charlie" Meadows, who started the first rodeo in 1885 at Payson, Arizona, and Juan Levais who was a cowboy that worked in and around Skull Valley. It is said that Buckey and his friend, Charles Genung, bet quite a bit of money on Horn to win the rodeo but in fact it was Juan Levais who won the first Prescott Rodeo. Horn, Meadows and Levais competed against each other at the Payson Rodeo, which was called August Doins and the rodeo in Globe over the next three to four years. Each of them were either first, second or third in all of those rodeos.

Tom Horn was born near Memphis, Scotland County, Missouri, on November 21, 1860. He was the fifth child of a family of twelve siblings. At the age of fourteen he ran away from home and ended up in Santa Fe, New Mexico, where he found work as a stagecoach driver for a local teamster. During this time period he learned to speak fluent Spanish. He bought his first gun, which was a Sharps fifty caliber rifle. Since he was too young to hang out at the bars he spent every free moment practicing with his rifle. After a couple of years of practicing every day, Horn became very proficient with his rifle. He became one of the best long range shooters in the territory. He could hit a target from 600 to 1,000 yards.

In 1882 Horn joined the U.S. Army, again as a scout and took part in the Tupper-Rafferty-Enmedio fight in the State of Sonora, Mexico. The following year Horn was promoted to the Chief of Scouts since Al Sieber had to retire, due to being shot in the leg, an injury that left him disabled. Horn was in charge of the scouts in the Sierra Madre Apache expedition in 1885. The Apache stronghold was located the mountains, south of Douglass, Arizona and into the Mexican State of Sonora. The expedition was let by Brigadier General George Crook in 1885 but the trip was not successful as Geronimo decided not to surrender. In 1886 Horn again led the scouts and General Crook to meet with Geronimo to obtain his surrender but again Crook was not successful. Finally, at the end of 1886 he led a small company of scouts and two officers to Skeleton Canyon, located a few miles north of the Mexican border line in the New Mexico, Territory, the place where

Geronimo finally surrendered of 1886.

Late in the afternoon of his first day in office, Sheriff O'Neill made his first arrest. According to the Arizona Weekly Journal-Miner newspaper an article appeared on January 17, 1889, stating;

New sheriff makes First Arrest

"Sheriff O'Neill made his first arrest yesterday. The warrant for the arrest was served on a man named Schurley, who was recently employed as a baker at the Pioneer Hotel, in Prescott. He is charged with stealing articles from the Railroad Hotel at Prescott Junction, and was arrested at Peach Springs and is in the county jail awaiting his trial."

Another article appeared in the Arizona Weekly Journal-Miner also in the same publication that said the following;

Sheriff O'Neill Sending Tax Assessments

"Sheriff Buckey O'Neill and his deputies are sending out blank assessment forms to all of the taxpayers in the county to be filled out with a list of all taxable property. Further noted in each letter sent along with the assessment forms, it was noted that during the year there will be one or more legal notices of sheriff's sale of items that will be sold to pay overdue taxes. These items

will consist mostly of mining claims, mining equipment, cattle ranches, ranching equipment and livestock to pay overdue taxes that are owed to the county."

Chapter Nine

On the night of March 20, 1889, four masked men robbed the express car of the eastbound Atlantic & Pacific Railroad Number 2 passenger train at the Canyon Diablo Station located thirty miles east of Flagstaff, Arizona Territory.

The crime was serious as the express manager was threatened at gunpoint and the fleeing bandits fired on pursuing lawmen. if they were convicted as the Canyon Diablo Robbers the four men would face the death penalty as the Arizona Territorial Congress recently passed a law that robbing a train was a capital offense. Passing this law also indicated how much power the railroads had in our country at that time period.

This robbery served as the first test case for the new law that had been passed in late January of 1889 making train robbery as a capital crime punishable by death. Newspapers as far as New York City hailed Sheriff O'Neill and his deputies for their perseverance and their tenacity for pursuing the outlaws and bringing them to justice. The papers also hailed the territorial leaders for following through with the new law.

The following was taken from the official report filed by Sheriff Buckey O'Neill of the pursuit, capture of the Canyon Diablo Train Robbers, found in the Arizona Historical Journal, written by the first Arizona Historian, James McLintock, along with various supporting newspaper and the report filed by Winslow town Marshall Will Barnes and his Deputy Bill Broadbent, found in Barnes' book, "*Apaches and Longhorns.*"

Sheriff Buckey O'Neill arrived at his office at 8:00 on the morning of March 21, 1889. Already present at his office waiting for him when he arrived was his friend Tom Horn, who had been working at a ranch near the town of Globe, Arizona and just happened to be in Prescott that morning. Horn stopped by O'Neill's office to tell his friend that he was leaving Prescott and heading to go to Fort Apache, which was some 300 miles east of Prescott in the White Mountains to find work

Also waiting at the Sheriff's office that morning was Carl T. Holton, an A & P Special Railroad Detective from Texas. Holton had been in Prescott for a couple of weeks investigating the disappearance of railroad property outside of Wickenburg, Arizona.

Just a little after ten o'clock that morning a railroad messenger delivered a telegram to Sheriff O'Neill from the Canyon Diablo Railroad Station. It read as follows;

> "About half past ten o'clock last nights the coast bound passenger express on the Atlantic & Pacific Railroad was held up here by four masked and heavily armed men. The masked men entered the express car while the train was standing at the Canyon Diablo Train Station, covering Mr. Knickerbocker, Express Agent, with their pistols and compelled him to "shell out" all the money he had in the safe, which amounted to between $600 and $800 dollars. As there is usually several thousand dollars carried on the train, the company was lucky to get off so easy.

> *The passengers were not molested at all, neither they, or anyone else on the train except the messenger. Conductor W. D. Ross was in charge of the train and was not notified of the robbery until after the train left the Canyon Diablo Train Station.*

The Prescott Journal-Miner Newspaper declared after hearing about the reward posted by the railroad,

> *"The reward will no doubt be paid promptly, when the officers who are persistently following the trail of the robbers capture them and bring them to Prescott to stand trial."*

Sheriff O'Neill turned directly to Horn and asked him if he wanted a job? Horn volunteered his services, so Buckey hired Horn on the spot as a special deputy tracker; Horn was immediately sworn in that very morning before they departed. Sheriff O'Neill wanted Horn to lead his Apache scouts in the pursuit of the outlaws. Then O'Neill sent a telegram to Deputy James Black, who was in charge of Northern Yavapai County, whose office was in his Flagstaff office. He told Black that he, along with Railroad Detectives Holton and Tom Horn, were on their way to Flagstaff that very afternoon by train. The telegram said they would be in Flagstaff sometime the next morning, March 22, 1889. Deputy Black sent a wire back to the sheriff, stating that he was going to bring his deputy Ed St. Clair, a local Flagstaff photographer and reporter, who doubled as a deputy on occasion to accompany them in the pursuit.

The night of the robbery, Winslow Town Marshall Will C. Barnes and, his Deputy Marshall, William Broadbent were notified that thieves had burglarized his ranch at the mouth of Box Canyon on Chevelon Creek, a little south of the town of Two Guns and had made off with equipment and supplies from his ranch.

Barnes could read trail sign like Sherlock Holmes could sniff clues from the carpet of an empty house. He had been ten years in the Arizona Territory and won the Medal of Honor during the Apache Indian campaigns. Broadbent was foreman of Barnes' ranch. Barnes and Broadbent were on the move the first thing the next morning and when they arrived at Will's ranch they found the tracks indicating the outlaw horsemen had crossed Chevelon Creek on a crude raft, swimming their horses, the same method they used the same method to cross Clark Creek, six miles west. The tracks, alternately on dirt, mud, and snow, revealed that the right forefoot of one of the horses had been recently shod with a second-hand show from which the nail heads protruded and that the animal was somewhat oversized.

Another one of the set of tracks indicated that one of the other horses had also been hastily shod, with its hind foot track revealing a shoe was out of line with the hoof. And a set of the third horse tracks, Barnes noticed, was that of a *"side-winder,"* which was a pacing pony whose hoof marks were distinctive. Each track was followed by a small pile of dirt thrown back by the *"snap"* of the hoof, a peculiarity of pacer horses. With this information, coupled with the observations of several of Barnes neighbors, Barnes figured the horses' belonged to cowboys of the Hashknife Outfit of the Aztec Land and Cattle Company. The area headquarters located opposite the Mormon village of Saint Joseph on the Little Colorado River near Wolf Crossing.

Barnes and Broadbent decided further tracking in the still blinding snowstorm would be futile. So, they went back to Winslow and there they bedded down and fed their horses at Breed's Corral, ate supper at the Harvey House, and sent a wire to the Deputy Sheriff's office in Holbrook informing him of the burglary and the information gathered regarding where they left the bandits' trail.

While Barnes and his foreman were sleeping at Doc Demorest's Hotel in Winslow the next night, March 20, 1889, the A & P Eastbound No. 2 passenger train stopped at the Canyon Diablo Station, 24 miles west of Winslow to replenish its wood box supply. Four men came from the shadows of the section house, held the crew at gunpoint and forced open the express safe, taking about $7,000 in cash, pocket watches and a set of diamond ear rings from passengers.

The robbers were identified as four Hash-Knife cowboys by the ranch hands at the Barnes Ranch. They were identified as, William Sterin, John Halford, Daniel Harvick and J. J. Smith. They all had been working in different areas of the ranch and they left their camps individually over a period of nearly a week before rendezvousing on Chevelon Creek. Near Chevelon Creek they committed the burglary at the Barnes ranch, taking grain, food and personal items. They stopped near Box Canyon to lay further plans for the heist.

After the daring robbery and on the run the four men stopped, at a point around five miles south of the train station, near the town of Two Guns, and divided the train loot into reasonable piles. Smith took the earrings. He removed the diamonds from their settings and put them loose in his vest pocket. From there the bandits headed east toward Winslow. When they got about ten miles from Winslow they turned and headed northwest after crossing the railroad tracks along a trail that led them to the small town of Luepp. From there they followed along an old Navajo trail next to the edge of Canyon Diablo stopping at Wolf Trading Post to buy food, ammo and other supplies. The outlaws continued heading northwest toward Lees Ferry on the Colorado River.

At around one o'clock in the morning of March the 20th, Barnes and Broadbent were rousted from their sleep by a Western Union Dispatcher with the news of the Canyon Diablo Train Robbery. The dispatcher told them that it may have been the same four outlaws that burglarized the Barnes ranch the day before. Barnes and Broadbent were also foremen of the Barnes Ranch. The two law officers strapped on their forty-four caliber pistols, and grabbed their Winchester 30/30 lever action repeating rifles. Then they woke up the livery stable clerk, who sold them some extra ammo, and watered and fed their horses before he saddled and bridled them.

An A & P Yard Engineer hooked up an engine with a stock car and a caboose at the Winslow train yard. Barnes and Broadbent loaded up their gear and their horses in the stock car then they boarded the caboose and the special train took off for Canyon Diablo Train Station, which was located about thirty-five miles west of Winslow, a journey of forty minutes.

Luckily for the officers, the major snowstorm finally stopped and the night was clear, so the breath of man and horse hung in the air. About four inches of snow still lay on the ground. Barnes and Broadbent ate their breakfast at the railroad section house. After finishing their meal, they mounted their horses and followed the trail the robbers left in the snow. The trail, only a few hours old, was very visible due to the light from a full moon. By the time Barnes and Broadbent were on the outlaws trail no more than an hour the sun came out and the snow started melting, the mud and snow leaving an even easier trail for the lawmen to pursue, at that point Barnes stated to Broadbent,

> "Look at the tracks in the snow. Do you recognize them? These are the same son-of-a-bitches we chased all day yesterday. They doubled back and robbed the train."

Barnes and Broadbent followed the outlaws trail for about five miles and it looked like the outlaws were riding toward Flagstaff, then after a couple more hours of following their trail, the officers realized the bandits had gradually changed direction and were starting to head north toward Wolf's Crossing.

Just before noon the two law officers, following the bandits trail came upon what was left of their camp. The camp was littered with the remains of the fire they made from stopping to eat their breakfast, along with the officers finding chipped tins, crackers, coffee grounds, and half-burned Wells Fargo envelope and twine. Soon after being back on the outlaws trail after leaving their messy camp, Barnes and Broadbent nearly lost the robbers' trail. Their sign disappeared on a flat sandstone rock area. Broadbent was able to pick up the trail by finding a bright woolen thread hanging from a sage brush limb. Barnes' wrote in his official report saying;

> *"We read it like an open book. They had ridden their horses onto the rocks, cut an old Navajo saddle blanket to pieces, tied pieces of the blanket around each horse's hooves to muffle the sound of the horses going over the rocky terrain. At that point the bandits rode boldly off the rocks."*

An hour later Barnes and Broadbent picked up the outlaws trail on the other side of the sandstone as it was easy to see, since the ground was muddy from the snow that was melting, and again were back on the trail and in hot pursuit of the robbers. After nearly three days on the trail of the Canyon Diablo Robbery suspects, Barnes and Broadbent, were dead tired, half starved, their horses *"done in,"* so they decided to call off their pursuit. The officers followed the outlaws trail for six or eight more miles to make sure the outlaws were still heading north and had not swung about heading for either Winslow or Flagstaff. They found a railroad section gang. Barnes left Bill Broadbent with their horses at the section gang work site and rode a hand-car into Winslow to report his findings.

Upon arriving at his Marshal's office Barnes learned that reinforcements were on the way. There was a telegram sitting on his desk that said the new Sheriff of Yavapai County, Buckey O'Neill, along with a posse including, Deputy James Black, Special Deputy Ed St. Clair, Atlantic & Pacific Railroad Detectives, Carl Holton and Fred Fornuff, along with Tom Horn, were in route from Flagstaff and were going to pick up the trail at the point where Barnes and Broadbent ended the pursuit.

Once Sheriff O'Neill, his trackers, and his deputies reached the spot where the railroad hands were working late in the day on the 23rd of March, 1889, they easily picked up the trail of the bandits. According to Sheriff O'Neill's report, they spent the night there and got an early start after breakfast on the morning of March 24, 1889. Then after eating their breakfast they followed the trail left by Barnes and Broadbent who left ample piles of stones, broken sage brush and rags tied to yucca stalks so they could pick up the trail easily. By eight o'clock that morning Sheriff O'Neill and his posse were hot on the pursuit.

The sheriff and his posse stopped at Wolf Trading Post later that morning and picked up food, ammunition and other items they would need for the pursuit. Hermann Wolf was happy to help them. He told the sheriff that the four men passed by the post two days earlier. He went on to say that some of his employees overheard the robbers say they were going to head to Wahweap Canyon. The posse set out on the bandits trail once more, after replenishing their supplies.

Sheriff O'Neill and his posse met with Barnes and Broadbent who also had been back on the trail, on the Navajo Indian Reservation about ten miles from the Navajo town of Window Rock. Marshal Barnes told Sheriff O'Neill that he and Broadbent left Winslow after a day of rest and had been on the robbers trail a day's ride ahead of Buckey and his posse. Barnes told O'Neill that he thought they were about a half day's ride from catching up to the robbers and by all the evidence their trail definitely led toward Wahweap Canyon on the Arizona and Southern Utah border.

Together the posse, now including Barnes and Broadbent, reached the outskirts of the Town of Window Rock on the evening of March 26, 1889. They ate a well-deserved dinner at a restaurant in Window Rock and after two days of hard riding the sheriff decided to rest his horses and men for the night, so they spent the night at a hotel in Window Rock. Sheriff O'Neill told the posse after dinner that they would need a good night's rest. He went on to say that the next day they would be covering as much ground as possible to make up the distance between them and the robbers. O'Neill told his posse that if they did not pursue the outlaws with great vigor that the robbers would continue to keep too much ground between them. The sheriff and his posse rose early the next morning. They ate a hearty breakfast and obtained more ammunition and supplies, hoping to catch the outlaws before they reached the Utah border.

Below is an article that appeared in the Albuquerque Democrat Newspaper on March 27, 1889, which indicates the boldness of the Canyon Diablo Train Robbers.

I Forgot My Gun

The four fellows who held up the Atlantic & Pacific Express Passenger Train on March 20, 1889, were cool ones. They left the express car and went away a short distance when, to the dismay of everyone, one of them went back and told Mr. Knickerbocker, the express messenger, that he had left his gun in the car and would like to get it. He stepped gaily into the compartment, secured the valuable weapon, lifted his had politely, then he bowed stating goodnight to the astonished messenger who wondered to this very day what ailed him, asking himself why he did not shoot the robber. Indeed, there is a question apropos of the whole affair, why did not the messenger shoot when the bandits started away, and why did he not shoot when one returned alone? Some of the men there were put in charge of the Wells Fargo & Company express treasure, and who were not afraid of a freebooter on earth, and a little blood spilling was indulged in on the part of the train hands, and messengers, the mountain roads would soon be free of the bold bandits."

After questioning a Navajo woman just outside of Window Rock early that morning, as she was herding sheep, Sheriff O'Neill and his posse learned from the woman, that the four men carried off one of her sheep. She said she found the carcass where they had killed and dressed it that very morning. Sheriff O'Neill thanked Barnes and Broadbent for their tenacity in trailing the robbers but dismissed them saying,

> *"I think we have enough fire power to bring in these robbers. You two can go on back to Winslow to get back to your local law officer duties. He went on to tell them he would be sure to include the two in his report so they would be paid for their expenses and their time."*

Sheriff O'Neill asked Marshall Barnes and Deputy Broadbent to stop by the railhead on their way into town and send a telegram to all of the settlements in and around northern Arizona and southern Utah to be on the lookout for the four robbers and that they were well armed and very dangerous.

According to Sheriff O'Neill, the robbers trail was not hard to follow. There was a light layer of snow still on the ground and with the information about the two unique hoof prints that two of the four horses left, it helped make the robbers trail easy to track. Sheriff O'Neill said the posse rode hard over the next two days hoping to make up the distance between them and the outlaws.

Sheriff O'Neill further stated that the posse followed the outlaw's trail to Lees Ferry on the

Colorado River located about twenty-five miles south of the Utah border. On the morning of March 31, 1889, O'Neill wrote the posse reached Lees Ferry at mid-day and they learned from an employee working the raft that the robbers had crossed over the river on the raft in the late afternoon on the previous day, March 30, 1889. The employee manning the raft told the sheriff and his posse, that it looked like they were headed north toward Wahweap Canyon just north of the Arizona Border in Southern Utah, near the Mormon settlement of Cannonville, Utah.

The above is a picture of Wahweap Canyon in the background past the Colorado River as it looked in 1889 was found in our National Archives.

When the posse reached the mouth of Wahweap Canyon they found tracks that looked like the robbers turned and headed south. The sheriff and Tom Horn figured the robbers were hoping to confuse their trackers by it looking like they doubled back. But then not far up the trail from the posse came across the carcass of a slaughtered steer the robbers rustled from a nearby ranch. Not far from the remains of the steer they found the remnants of a campfire where the robbers stopped to cook the meat and eat it for dinner the previous night. The campfire was still warm when the posse reached it, indicating that the outlaws were a few hours ahead of them, according to Tom Horn.

Unbeknownst to the Sheriff and his posse, the citizens from the Town of Cannonville, after receiving the telegram regarding the robbers, found them just outside of their town. They snuck up on the robbers and surrounded them and tried to hold them for the sheriff and his posse, but one of the robbers got the drop on the townspeople and disarmed all of them. The robbers took their weapons, ammo, fresh mounts and were back on the run within an hour of the time they were supposedly captured.

Just before nightfall that same evening of the 31st of March Deputy Jim Black caught a glimpse of one of the robbers riding in the distance. He shouted to the man to stop. The man kept riding and fired a shot back at the posse. Deputy Black jumped off his horse and grabbed his rifle. He took close aim and fired one shot hitting and killing the horse the robber was riding. The robber ran away on foot and jumped on the back of one of his companion's horse. None of the posse was able to get off another shot so the men fled with the posse hot on their tail.

Having two men on one horse slowed the robbers get-away. The posse was able to catch them fairly quickly. The robbers knew the posse was close so they set a trap to ambush their pursuers. When they opened fire on the posse when the men got close, one of the robbers hit Sheriff O'Neill's horse, killing him instantly. Sheriff O'Neill was pinned under the horse and was a dead meat target. Railroad Detective Holton went to the aide of the sheriff and rescued him under duress of several volleys of shots coming from the robbers. The posse fired back at the bandits from the cover of rocks while helping to provide the needed cover for Holton and Sheriff O'Neill. Railroad Detective Holton was able to pull the sheriff to safety amidst several more volleys of shots fired at them.

The robbers somehow slipped by the posse and made their escape, again. It was not long though before the posse caught up with the robbers and again was engaged in another running firefight. Luckily during this fight none of the posse was injured, but two of the outlaws were wounded during the firefight. Somehow though, the robbers made their escape, once again. At this point Buckey O'Neil and his posse's horses were done in from the long pursuit. With fresh mounts the posse could have easily captured the escaping, injured robbers. But it was imperative at this point to obtain new mounts in order to continue the pursuit. The nearest ranch was twenty miles away, close to the Utah-Arizona, States border.

The posse headed for the nearby ranch to obtain fresh mounts. When they arrived, the rancher informed the posse that he had heard the town's people from Cannonville had surrounded the outlaws in hopes of holding them until you and your posse arrived. But he went on to say that, somehow the outlaws got the upper hand on the town's people and ended up with all of their guns, sending their pursuers away on foot; effectively taking their fresh horses, guns, ammo and food and escaping unharmed.

Below is a newspaper article that appeared in the Prescott Journal-Miner on April 3, 1889, regarding the sheriff and his posse in the pursuit and capture of the Canyon Diablo Train Robbers;

SHERIFF O'NEILL AND POSSE IN HOT PURSUIT

"A gentleman who arrived on last night's train from Holbrook, reports that Sheriff O'Neill and his deputies were only five miles behind the A & P Railroad Train Robbers. The sheriff's posse had fresh mounts of horses, while the horses ridden by the robbers were pretty well worn out. The chances of their capture were good unless something unforeseen should happen. Sheriff O'Neill sent a telegram to Sheriff McInernay in Winslow stating that his posse was in hot pursuit and that nothing would be gained by sending another posse. He went on to say he felt the robbers capture was soon imminent."

The next morning, April 1, 1889, after a night of rest and their bellies full from a hearty breakfast,

Sheriff O'Neill and his posse were hot after the outlaws after obtaining fresh mounts. They reached the robbers that morning in a heavily wooded area near the Mormon settlement of St. George, Utah. They called on the men to surrender, and were answered with a volley of shots from the outlaws' six shooters, with which they were well armed. The terrain now consisted of a dense Aspen forest, with down trees, so both parties were well protected and a pitched battle ensued, during which one of the robbers had his cartridge belt literally shot from his gun belt, another outlaw had a bullet hole in his hat, and some of their horses were killed in the firefight.

After fifteen minutes of constant shooting from both sides, the robbers concluded it was getting too hot for them, leaving their horses they made a hasty retreat on foot. The country was covered with dense growth and underbrush, but the persistent officers soon overhauled one of the robbers, William "Billy" Steiren, a noted desperado, and thought to be the leader of the gang.

The next morning as the posse sat around the fire eating breakfast, Sheriff O'Neill decided to go ahead and see if the outlaws were close. He thought he heard a noise coming from a short distance ahead of their camp on the trail, before they went to sleep the night before.

> "Hello boys, what's new?" When they reached for their guns, he told them, "No you don't! Put your hands in the air, and kick those guns over toward me. If you go for those guns I will kill all three of you where you stand."

For one full hour O'Neill held the desperados under his guns while he waited for his posse to catch up to him. Once the rest of his men arrived and they put the men in handcuffs and under arrest, O'Neill secured all of their saddlebags. After going through all of their bags, low and behold concealed in one of the Wells Fargo marked bags, obviously taken from the train robbery, was $350,000. The loss Atlantic & Pacific Railroad had initially indicated was of no real consequence. There was also evidence found in the baggage indicating that they were the same robbers that held up another A&P Passenger Railroad Train several months' earlier at the Bellemont Train Station.

Continuing the personal search of each outlaw the posse found, besides the large sum of money that was still in Wells Fargo envelopes, gold coins and watches. The diamonds that J. J. Smith removed from their settings and placed in the pocked of his vest were never found. After being questioned at great length, Smith later admitted,

> *"All I can figure is that I probably scraped tobacco crumbs from my pockets and put them in my pipe along with the diamonds that I stuck in the same vest pocket and when I finished smoking my pipe, I tapped the ashes out on the ground along with the gems and I did not realize that the diamonds were missing until you officers searched me."*

The posse also found in the robbers' saddle bags some clothing and razors that came from the burglary at the Barnes Ranch. Sheriff O'Neill and his posse had all four bandits, most of the loot from the express box and enough additional evidence to convince a grand jury of his prisoners' guilt in the Barnes Robbery and the two Atlantic & Pacific Train Robberies.

The photo above of the area where the firefight took place and the outlaws were captured was found on the United States Forest service website.

Chapter Ten

The pursuit had taken a full two weeks but the young sheriff and his posse had finally succeeded in catching and arresting their prey in a remote canyon in southern Utah, definitely out of Sheriff Buckey O'Neill's Yavapai County, Arizona Territory and his jurisdiction. From which another difficulty arose. Returning with their prisoners over the 300 miles they had come would be no easy undertaking, and would provide too many opportunities for the prisoners to escape. After deliberating over the problem the sheriff and his posse decided to press on to the nearest railroad station in Marysvale, Utah, and from there they would transport the prisoners by train back to Prescott.

On the way to Marysvale, the posse stopped at the town of Panguich, Utah. There they commissioned a blacksmith to make hand cuffs and leg irons to shackle the prisoners with, while they rode onto Marysvale. The blacksmith rigged the foot shackles to connect under the horse's belly so the robbers would not be able to get off their horses without the officers unhooking them. He also made the hand cuffs and shackles so that the robbers could ride their horses but each robber was connected with chains. After a 300-mile pursuit Sheriff O'Neill wanted to make sure the prisoners could not escape while riding their mounts to the train station. The shackles would also prevent the men from escaping from the train, during the long trip back to Prescott.

The group continued from Panguich, Utah traveling up the trail next to the Sevier River to the Town of Marysvale, Utah. On the evening of April 10, 1889, the party reached Salt Lake City, Utah, by the Union Pacific Passenger train they boarded at the Marysvale train station. Once Sheriff O'Neill had secured the prisoners in the city jail; he prepared, submitted, and filed the extradition papers needed to allow him and his posse to transport the prisoners back from Utah to Arizona.

The posse remained in Salt Lake City for three days, while awaiting the extradition papers to arrive. While they were there, they prepared their arrangements to transport the prisoners back to Prescott to stand trial. Once they received the extradition papers in Salt Lake City, since there was no direct train service from Salt Lake City to Prescott, the posse and prisoners continued on to Denver, Colorado, where they started the long trip home by train from Denver back to Prescott. From Denver their first stop would be Santa Fe, New Mexico, then Albuquerque, New Mexico, then to Flagstaff, Arizona. From Flagstaff they would go to Ashfork, and from there onto their destination of Prescott, Arizona. From Marysvale, Utah, to Prescott, Arizona, they would have to travel a total of 900 miles by rail.

While the posse was waiting there in Salt Lake City for the extradition papers, Sheriff O'Neill sent a message to Prescott to let them know that he and his posse had captured the Canyon Diablo Train Robbers and would be on their way back to Prescott with their captured outlaws. Territorial Governor Louis Wolfley sent O'Neill and his posse a congratulatory telegram:

> "To William O. Buckey O'Neill, Prescott, Arizona. I, Arizona Governor Louis Wolfley, the undersigned, most heartily congratulate you on your successful capture of the train robbers after so persistent and dangerous a trip. The people of Arizona and the country in general are proud of your achievement."

While Sheriff O'Neill and his posse were in Salt Lake City, awaiting the extradition papers, with outlaws safely in jail, the posse had their picture taken. The day they arrived at Salt Lake City, Railroad Detective Fornouff received orders to leave immediately to investigate another train robbery. Sheriff O'Neill knew that he had to keep expenses as low as possible. Since he was out of his jurisdiction and the expenses regarding a chase that took two weeks from the start until the robbers were captured, so he dismissed Deputy Tom Horn, since his job of tracking was over. Sheriff O'Neill figured his Deputy James Black, along with Special Deputy Ed St. Clair, and Railroad Detective Carl T. Holton, and of course, he, would be enough men to transport the robbers back to Prescott, especially since they were traveling by train.

Below and on the following two pages is a newspaper article that appeared in the San Francisco Chronicle on April 11, 1899, regarding the capture of the Canyon Diablo Train Robbers:

TRAIN ROBBERS CAPTURED

Particulars of the Capture

"A telegram of the 10th instant from Salt Lake is published in the San Francisco Chronicle on the 11th, announcing the arrival in the former place of Sheriff O'Neill and his posse with the train robbers, giving some particulars of their capture. The sheriff's party consisted of Sheriff O'Neill, and his Deputy James L. Black, of Flagstaff, Special Deputy Ed St. Clair of the same place, and Carl T. Holton, special detective for the Atlantic & Pacific Railroad. After a chase of 600 miles over high mountains, parched plains, during which the officers suffered many privations, the robbers were sighted on April 1, 1889, nearly two weeks from the start of the pursuit, in Wahweap Canyon, about forty miles east of Cannonsville, Utah. The officers called on the men to surrender and were answered with a volley from their six-shooters, with which they were well armed. The country being heavily timbered, both parties were well protected and a pitched battle ensued, during which one of the robbers actually had his cartridge box, shot off of his belt, another had a bullet hole put through his hat, and several of their horses were killed. About fifty shots having been exchanged, with the result above stated, the robbers concluded it was getting too hot for them and leaving their horses they beat a hasty retreat on foot.

The country is covered with a dense growth of underbrush, which made the pursuit very tedious, but the officers persisted and soon overhauled Bill Stiren, a noted desperado and probably the leader of the gang. The next day outlaws, Charlie Clark, John Smith, and James Quince were captured by the sheriff and his posse. They had now succeeded in their object but another difficulty arose. To return their prisoners over the road they had come would be no easy undertaking, and after consideration, it was decided to press on to Marysvale, Utah, and then go to Denver by way of Salt Lake City and then take the Santa Fe Railroad through Albuquerque, New Mexico, then from there to Flagstaff, then on to Ashfork and then back down to Prescott, Arizona.

On the way up to Salt Lake City one of the prisoners made a full confession, so that there is not the slightest doubt as to the right men having been captured. A funny incident is related in connection with an attempt made by the citizens of Cannonsville to arrest the men. Shortly before the arrival of the officers, eight armed men with a small army of followers undertook the job. The robbers waited quietly until the citizens were near enough, when they suddenly covered the citizens with their guns and made them stack their arms and depart. Strange to say all of the prisoners are well educated, and Smith claims to be the son of a Baptist Minister. Officer Holton says he formerly knew Stiren in New Mexico, where he trained with a hard gang and was generally considered a bad man. Their ages are; Clark 25, Quince 28, Smith 28, and Stiren around 30.

> The men were quite jolly when arrested, but they are beginning to realize their position now and show signs of drooping. Train robbing was made a capital offense by the last Arizona Legislature, and as the court site in June, they are in a fair way to reap the reward which their villainy merits. The party left for Denver this afternoon, and will arrive in Prescott on Tuesday night."

At this point, the author will discuss the background regarding the passing of the law making train robbery a capital offense. Individual states at various times throughout American History have embraced shifting definitions of what constitutes a crime punishable by death. In 1928, for example, the Massachusetts Penal Code listed six capital crimes, including burglary, robbery and arson. South Carolina punished dozens of crimes by death; by 1850 its' code still contained twenty-two capital offenses.

The often lengthy list of capital crimes concocted by some states, prior to the Civil War, stemmed from three general causes, first, and perhaps most relevant, was the simple fact that many states still used portions of the Old English Penal Code, which during the 1700's contained 222 crimes punishable by death. While the American Colonies and later states never went to this extreme, many, such as South Carolina, remained heavily influenced by English Common Law. A second related reason, for the high number of capital offenses, stemmed from a general belief that severity of punishment was the best deterrent of crime. Finally, most antebellum states lacked an effective prison system. Therefore, many localities defended capital punishment because there was no suitable alternative.

By the time Arizona became a Territory in 1863, the birth of a coherent penitentiary system and the work of reformers reduced the number of crimes punishable by death. The law even brought about abolishment of the death penalty in some states. Arizona's first penal code was heavily influence by these reforms, and for most of the territorial era, the only crimes punishable by death were treason, first-degree murder and like all states in the U. S., stealing a horse was a hanging offense. Then robbing a train was added to most states list.

The two most commonly used justifications for the death penalty have been retribution and deterrence. Proponents of the death penalty have argued that it provides a notice to upright citizens that the criminal has paid for his crime in full measure, and that the wrong has been avenged, and that justice has been served. Moreover, the threat and media spectacle of an execution, particularly prior to 1900 when many executions were public events, has been regarded as an effective warning to would be offenders.

Since train robberies could be cold-blooded, it is understandable that legislatures might want to add them to the list of crimes punishable by death. For example, a particularly notorious holdup occurred in 1896, when bandits loosened the rail on the Louisville and Nashville track at its' approach to a bridge over the Cahaba River in Alabama.

Twenty-seven of the thirty-five passengers, and three crew members, were killed when the train plunged 110 feet into the river below. Immediately after the wreck, the robbers went through the cars robbing the dead and injured. Needless to say, robberies that resulted in the deaths of passengers or train employees, such as the Cahaba River Robbery or the Pixley Robbery which prefaced the passage of Arizona's capital punishment law reasonably fell within the group of crimes contemporary Arizonans though should be punishable by death. After all, first degree murder was a capital crime in the Arizona Territory. It was logical, then, that a homicide committed during the act of robbing a train should also be punishable by death. The crime clearly fit within this context, but what about train robberies that did not result in a homicide?

Not all train robberies were equal in terms of the harm they inflicted. In fact, most train robbers in American History avoided injuring passengers or railroad employees. Clearly, by making train robberies a capital offense, death penalty supporters in Arizona and elsewhere were not simply seeking to make the punishment equal to the crime; they were seeking to deter future criminal activity.

On the next two pages is an article also written by a reporter from the Prescott Arizona Weekly Journal-Miner newspaper that was published on Wednesday April 17, 1889. This article is important since it explains and verifies the fact that the law had passed making train robbery in Arizona a capital offense;

DEATH PENALTY FOR TRAIN ROBBERY

"The bill passed by the Fifteenth Arizona Territorial Legislature making train robbing punishable by death, and which received the signature of the governor, and is now the law of this territory, was introduced by Honorable Lew Martin, of Pima County, a railroad engineer on the Southern Pacific Railroad. The New Mexico Legislature at its session two years ago passed a similar law, since when, no train robbery has occurred in that territory. The following is the full text of the Arizona Law, being the second bill introduced in the house, defining certain offenses against the public peace, when it is enacted by the Legislative Assembly of the Territory of Arizona:

Section 1: If any person or persons shall willfully and maliciously make any assault upon any railroad train, railroad cars, or railroad locomotives, within the territory, for the purpose and with the intent to commit murder, robbery or any other felony upon or against any engineer, conductor, fireman, brakeman or any officer or employee connected with the said locomotive, train or cars, or any express messenger or mail agent on the train, or in any of the cars thereof, upon conviction thereof, shall be deemed guilty of a felony, and shall suffer the punishment of death.

Section 2: Any and all persons, who shall counsel, aid, abet and assist in the perpetration of the offense or of the offenses set forth in the preceding section, on convincing thereof shall, suffer the punishment herein prescribed.

Section 3: Upon the trial of any and all persons charged with violation of this act, it shall be deemed material to a conviction, that the defendants specifically intended to commit the offense, or any of them, herein set forth, upon or against any particular person, but it shall be sufficient if it is proven to the satisfaction of the court and jury trying the cause, as the result of such unlawful assault, some person or persons was killed, robbed or injured, as the case may be, or that such assault was perpetrated with the design to commit some felony.

Section 4: This act shall be in full force from and after its passage and shall be in effect immediately after this legislature adjourns.

Below is another nationally syndicated newspaper article that was published and appeared in the New Orleans, Louisiana Daily Picayune newspaper on Friday April 12, 1889. The Article was originally published on April 11, 1889 by the Salt Lake Herald including the published picture of the officers taken in Salt Lake City.

Tracked and Taken

The Canon Diablo Train Robbers Arrested in Utah

After a sharp engagement with the Sheriff's Posse

The Crime fully confessed by One of the Outlaws

The Offense Punishable by the

Death Penalty Under the Arizona Law

Salt Lake City, Utah, April 11, 1889- The four Arizona Officers, pictured below, who arrived here yesterday with the four train robber's in custody tell an interesting story of the long chase.

On March 21, 1889 an Atlantic and Pacific train was stopped at Canon Diablo, Yavapai County, Arizona, for orders, when the men boarded the engine and persuaded the fireman and the engineer, with revolvers to order the express messenger to open his car. This was done. Then the robbers,

They Broke Open the Strong Box

And after securing all the money in it, struck south toward the Tonto Basin and then they proceeded as far in that direction to Sunset Mountain, when they turned north and headed for Utah.

Sheriff O'Neill is pictured second from the right, the Sheriff of Yavapai County was notified and along with Special A & P Railroad Agent Carl Holton, second from the left, Deputy Sheriff James L Black, on the far right and Deputy Sheriff Ed St. Clair, pictured on the far left, started in pursuit. They trailed the robbers nearly 300 miles north from the road to as wild and desolate country.

The picture of the arresting officers on the next page was taken in Salt Lake City while they were awaiting the extradition papers to transport the outlaws back to Prescott to stand trial. This picture was found on the Pinterest website.

It was a dangerous trip too, for the region is infested with desperados, whose sympathies were all with the pursued party. At last, after a journey of over 600 miles, crossing the little and main Colorado Rivers, over high mountains and parched plains, during which the officers suffered many privations, the robbers were sighted on April 1, 1889, nearly two weeks after the robbery, in Wahweep Canon, located about forty miles east of Canonville, Utah. The officers called on the men to surrender and were answered with,

A Volley from their Revolvers

Of which they were armed. The country being heavily wooded, both parties were well protected. A battle ensued in which one of the robbers had his cartridge box shot from his belt, another had a bullet hole put through his hat, and one of their horses was killed. After about fifty shots had been exchanged, the robbers concluded it was getting too warm for them, and leaving their horses, they beat a hasty retreat on foot.

The country is covered with a dense growth of underbrush, which rendered pursuit very difficult; but the officers persisted and overtook Bill Stineau, a noted desperado and probably the leader of the gang. The next day Charles Clark and John Smith were captured, and on April 4th, James Quince was captured.

The officers had now succeeded in their object, but another difficulty presented itself. To return with the prisoners over the same road they had come would be,

No Small Undertaking

and after considerations it was decided to press on to Milford, Utah, and then go to Denver by way of Salt Lake and from there take the Santa Fe Railroad back to Prescott.

It is not known, even by the officers, how much money was stolen, but that found on them, together with what had been accounted for, amounts to a thousand dollars. On the way up, one of the prisoners made a full confession, so that there is not the slightest doubt that the right parties had been captured.

A funny incident is related in an attempt by the citizens of Canonville to arrest the men. Shortly before the arrival of the officers, eight armed men with a small army of followers undertook this job. The robbers waited quietly until the citizens were near enough, when they covered them with their guns, then they left. All of the prisoners are well educated and J.J. Smith claims to be the son of a Baptist minister.

A & P Special Officer Carl T. Holton says he formerly knew Stineau in New Mexico, where he trained with a hard gang and was generally considered bad.

Below is a typical ranch in settlement of Cannonville Utah aka; the gateway to Bryce Canyon National Park, was found in our National Archives

Chapter Eleven

The following is Sheriff O'Neill's account of the capture of the Canyon Diablo Train Robbers, as told to the Salt Lake Herald reporter who wrote this story. This newspaper article was a nationally syndicated article that was also published in the San Francisco Chronicle on Wednesday April 10, 1889. Some of this information is a repeat of the information already presented but it is a good well written article and explains further some of the facts of the robbery and the outlaws who were captured.

Canyon Diablo Train Robbers Are Captured

"There was a great crowd that had gathered the morning we arrived at the Salt Lake City train depot. Word had been sent ahead of our arrival date. The people were waiting at the Utah Central Depot that morning expecting to see the Arizona Train Robbers and their captors. They were not disappointed, for four robbers in the charge of four Arizona law officers arrived at the station on time.

The prisoners were heavily ironed, these useful ornaments having been riveted on by a blacksmith in Panguich, Utah. The robbers were taken to the City jail at once. From there the officers proceeded to a local hotel to clean up and rest after the long two weeks of pursuing the robbers over the roughest terrain imaginable.

Sheriff Buckey O'Neill of Prescott, Arizona Territory, when interviewed by this correspondent said: 'This past March 21st an Atlantic and Pacific Passenger Train that was stopped to refill wood at the Canyon Diablo train station in Yavapai County, Arizona Territory.

While the train was being refilled with wood and taking on water, four men boarded the train with their six-shooters covering him, persuaded the fireman to take them to the express messenger and then forced the express manager to open the door to the express car.

After this was done, the robbers then broke open the strong box and secured all the money in it, then they struck south toward the town of Two Guns and then after passing the town they struck east toward the town of Winslow, then they turned north toward Utah.'

Sheriff O'Neill stated he was notified the next morning of the affair. Along with Railroad Detectives Holton and St. Clair, Tom Horn their tracker and the Sheriff himself. They boarded their horse, placed their supplies on a train and then they proceeded north to Ashfork, then on to Flagstaff where they met Deputy Sheriff James L. Black and Railroad Special Agent Ed St. Clair at Yavapai County's northern office. From there they started the pursuit of the robbers. A better posse could not have been selected, as those composing it are men of the highest courage, and are thoroughly familiar with the country. The posse trailed the robbers for over 300 miles, from the line of the railroad, through as wild and desolate a country as can be found in the west, it was a dangerous trip, too, for the region is infested with desperados whose sympathy is all with the pursued party as they are all well known by folks in that part of the territory.

At last after a hard journey of more than 300 miles, crossing the Little and Main Colorado Rivers, over high mountains, parched plains, during which the officers suffered many privations, the robbers were sighted on April 1st, nearly two weeks after the affair in Wahweap Canyon, which is located about forty miles east of the Mormon village of Cannonville in Northern Yavapai County.

The officers called on the men to surrender, and were answered with a volley of shots from the robbers' six-shooters, with which they were well armed. That part of the country was heavily wooded. Both parties were well protected and a pitched firefight ensued, during which one of the robbers had his cartridge box shot from his belt, another had a bullet hole put through his hat, and some of their horses were killed.

After a total of about fifty shots had been exchanged by both parties, with the result above stated, the robbers concluded it was getting too hot for them, and leaving their horses they beat a hasty retreat on foot. The country is covered with dense growth of underbrush, which made the pursuit very tedious, but the officers persisted and soon overhauled Bill Steiren, a noted desperado, thought to be the leader of the gang. The next day John Smith and Charles Clark were captured and the following day the last robber, James Quince was captured.

The posse had finally succeeded in their object, but another difficulty arose. To return with their prisoners over the same trail they had come would not be an easy undertaking, so it was decided after much consideration to press on to the town of Milford, Utah, which was the closest railroad station and from there to travel to Salt Lake City by way of the Central Utah Railway and from Salt Lake City to Denver then take the Santa Fe Railroad back to Prescott.

The prisoners were quite gay during the trip until we started from Milford to Salt Lake City, then after being informed of the new law that had been passed that would send them to the gallows for train robbery the prisoners changed their tune and made full confessions, so that there is not the slightest doubt the posse caught the right men having been captured.

A funny incident that I have already mentioned was related to this reporter in connection with an attempt made by *the citizens of Cannonville in an attempt to arrest the robbers near their village in Wahweap Canyon. Shortly before the arrival of the officers, eight armed men with a small army of followers undertook this job. The robbers waited quietly until the citizens were near enough, when they jumped from hiding in the trees and suddenly covered the citizens with their guns and made them stack their arms and ammunition, then the robbers sent the citizens back to their village.*

As this reporter also interviewed the prisoners upon their arrival at the Salt Lake Train Station and it was obvious the men were well educated. Smith claimed to be the son of a Baptist minister. Railroad Detective Holton told this reporter that he had crossed paths with William Steiren previously in New Mexico. Holton said Steiren trained a hard gang of cutthroats. He was considered a bad hombre. Their ages are: Clark 25, Quince 28, Smith 27 and Steiren about 30 years of age.

The sheriff told this reporter the men were quite jolly when they were first arrested in the beginning, but then after being told about the passing of the new law that made train robbing a capital offense they soon lost their spirit and confessed to the officers hoping that it would soften their sentence. The party left Salt Lake City today and is scheduled to arrive in Prescott Tuesday night."

The Atchison Topeka and Santa Fe Railway Train carrying the Sheriff, his posse and the prisoners, left Denver late on the afternoon of April 10, 1889 and headed south toward Albuquerque with its first stop at Trinidad, Colorado, that was just north of the New Mexico-Colorado border.

From Trinidad, the train travels 194 miles to its next stop that is at Santa Fe and from there to Albuquerque, New Mexico. After filling their tender with wood at the Trinidad Train Station they proceeded south about 25 miles, when they reached Raton Pass at 10 o'clock that evening. Just before they started the 12 mile descent of the steep pass that drops close to 2400 feet, Sheriff O'Neill made one more pass to make sure the prisoners were secure and found them all sleeping. He knew the train would gather speed so he wanted to be sure the prisoners were secure before the train started down the pass.

Sheriff O'Neill decided they would take two hour shifts watching the prisoners. He and Deputy St. Clair took the first watch while Deputy Black and Railroad Detective Holton slept. At about midnight Sheriff O'Neill and Deputy St. Clair woke up Black and Holton to take their turn watching the prisoners while he and St. Clair got a well-deserved couple of hours of sleep.

Deputy Black and Railroad Detective Holton must have still been tired because they fell asleep. While the two guards were sleeping, J. J. Smith figured out a way to remove the shackles from his boots and then the chains attached to the shackles that secured him to the train car floor. He slipped his foot out of his boot, and made his escape by opening a window and squeezing through it as the train slowed down.

Somehow Sheriff O'Neill heard the commotion and discovered that Smith had escaped and his deputies were asleep. One of the prisoners described his reaction as he pulled the cord to stop the train;

> "His language loud enough to thoroughly awaken his deputies was fluent and to the point, a great mass of language, not all profane, that seemed to be almost overcoming him."

Deputy St. Clair was left behind to guard the remaining three prisoners while Sheriff O'Neill, Deputy Black and Detective Holton left the train to track and try to recapture the escaped prisoner J.J. Smith, in the dark. They were at a major disadvantage as it was pitch dark, so after a six-hour pursuit, they returned to the train and the train proceeded down the track to take the remaining three prisoners to Prescott to stand trial.

Railroad Detective Holton told Sheriff O'Neill that when they had the three prisoners secured in Prescott that he would take the next train back to the place where Smith escaped and trail him until he found him. He told Sheriff O'Neill that it looked by the tracks that Smith was heading back to Texas. He told O'Neill that he was responsible for the prisoner escaping and that after wiring all of the law offices between Raton Pass and West Texas that he would eventually catch Smith.

The posse with the three prisoners secured on the train went ahead and headed back through Santa Fe, then Albuquerque, from there they changed trains and caught a westbound Santa Fe train to Flagstaff, from there to Ashfork and then from Ashfork southeast to Prescott for prosecution.

Below is a photo of the train carrying Buckey O'Neill, standing in the train doorway and they take the last leg from Ashfork to Prescott to trial arraignment. Notice the guards are now taking this job very seriously. This photo was also found in our National Archives.

On April 15, 1889, Sheriff Buckey O'Neill and his posse arrived at the Prescott Train Station. They were dead tired from guarding the three prisoners from Denver to Prescott, but finally the prisoners were in their cells in the Prescott Yavapai County Jail.

In their preliminary hearing, the captives faced several formidable witnesses. The first was the A & P Railroad Express Manager, E.G. Knickerbocker, whose safe had been robbed at the

Canyon Diablo Station, then Sheriff O'Neill, followed by Deputies James Black, Bill Broadbent and Will Barnes.

After the preliminary testimonies were presented, the judge found enough evidence to hold the prisoners for a grand jury trial. Before the trial though, the three outlaws agreed to a plea bargain and plead guilty to armed train robbery and the three were each sentenced to 25-year terms at the Yuma Territorial Prison, in lieu of going to trial where they could possibly receive the death penalty. Sadly, for them the new law had been passed on March 6, 1889, just two weeks before they decided to rob the A&P Passenger Train at Canyon Diablo on March 21, 1889.

Below is another newspaper article from the Arizona Weekly Journal-Miner on April 24, 1889. It brings to light more attention to the plight of the Canyon Diablo Robbers;

Train Robbers Brought Before Judge Fleury

"The Canyon Diablo Train Robbers were brought before Superior Court Judge Fleury for their first appearance on the charges of reckless endangerment and train robbery. The court attorney was not ready and the case was continued for a week. One of the prisoners, John Halford, who is currently in the Yavapai County jail, is being treated for a gunshot wound in his left leg that he received in one of the two running gun battles with Sheriff O'Neill and his posse.

> Deputy James Black and A&P Train Detective Carl T. Holton had discovered that escaped train robber, J. J. Smith, had stolen a horse and was headed for Texas. They sent a telegram to Sheriff O'Neill stating they were close to apprehending the leader of the train robbing gang.
>
> During the time the three prisoners were in jail waiting to be transported to the Yuma Territorial Prison, they found out that their fellow robber, J. J. Smith, had made it all the way to Vernon, Texas. Then on June 21, 1889, Sheriff O'Neill received a telegram indicating Smith had been recaptured, that he and Carl T. Holton were on their way back to Prescott."

After his daring leap from the train window, Smith made his way toward Texas just as Detective Holton, suspected, by stealing horses along the way and riding them as long as they would carry him. While traveling through the Texas Panhandle near the Town of Vernon, during the afternoon of his ninth day on run, Smith came across a woman wandering aimlessly across the prairie.

The woman told him that she had been lost and without food for two days. Smith now faced a dilemma. Not only was he on the lam for a capital crime, but he had drawn local attention to himself by stealing horses. His best chance for escape was to keep moving. However, it was clear to him that the young woman would not last much longer without assistance. Smith decided to take her to a windmill he had passed about eight miles back. After depositing the woman at the windmill, he followed a wire fence to a camp of men employed to maintain the fence. Smith notified them about the woman and then left.

Unfortunately for Smith, his chivalrous deed did not go unpunished. Sheriff J. T. Conn and a posse from Wilbarger County, Texas, were looking for Smith when they came across the ranch hands early the next morning. Based on their description, Conn knew that he was closing in on the Arizona train robber. Before noon, the Texas lawman overtook and cornered the fugitive. Smith, knowing he was looking at the death penalty opened fire on the posse and during the brief firefight he was shot in the left thigh and subsequently surrendered. When Sheriff Conn arrived back at his office he notified the railroad and Sheriff O'Neill that he had captured Smith. It so happened, that A & P Railroad Detective Holton and Deputy James Black were hot on Smith's trail. When he heard that Sheriff Conn had Smith in custody he left immediately to extradite the prisoner back to Prescott to stand trial.

Appearing in the Arizona Weekly Journal-Miner on June 21, 1889, the newspaper article below and on the next page verified the recapture of J. J. Smith;

THE BOSS TRAIN ROBBER

Recaptured by Carl Holton

"A special, of date June 21, from Vernon, Texas, to the Albuquerque Democrat, reads as follows:

Carl T. Holton and Deputy James Black have again captured J.J Smith, the Arizona Train Robber who escaped from them some weeks since jumping from the car window near Trinidad, Colorado.

There has never been known in the history of crime two such pursuits as have been given Smith since the robbery was committed on the Atlantic & Pacific Railroad, and there was never known a more daring and reckless escape than that which Smith affected by throwing himself shackled from the train car window, while the train was in motion.

Fugitives and detectives alike have found his match in the other. He stopped to help a woman who was lost in the desert and took her to a mine camp. The information from the miners at the camp was all that Holton and Black needed as they were already on his trail.

The race is now ended, and there can be but little hope in the part of the prisoner of any future escape."

Chapter Twelve

J. J. Smith's trial was notable for the strenuous efforts of his defense lawyer Robert Brown to free his client. Brown began his defense by attempting to quash the indictment on procedural grounds. His most significant argument was calling into question the use of U.S. District Court seals on paperwork filed in the Territorial District Court. Although the officials presiding over both courts were essentially the same, their jurisdictions were completely different. The train robbery case clearly fell under territorial law.

The importance of the issue was not missed by the Arizona Weekly Journal-Miner, which noted that;

> *"Should the question raised by Brown ever be sustained by the courts, the consequences would be far reaching."*

Not only would Smith have to be re-indicted, but because the seal had been used in the proceedings for both jurisdictions for years, hundreds of previous convictions could well have been placed in jeopardy. The court however, dismissed Brown's motion, along with his other attempts to free Smith on technicalities.

Brown then focused his attention on the merits of the case. He quickly realized though, that despite everything that had transpired, the evidence of Smith's participation in the Canyon Diablo holdup was completely circumstantial. No one had actually seen him rob the train; the sole witness to the crime, E. G. Knickerbocker, could only conclusively state that he had been robbed by four masked men. During that chilly, dark night, could he really be sure there were four outlaws?

The case against Smith became so tenuous that District Attorney H. D. Smith subpoenaed Halford, Stiren and Harvick to testify for the prosecution; forcing Sheriff O'Neill to transport the convicts back and forth to Yuma at a total cost of $1,000. Brown objected, claiming that the prisoners had struck a deal with the district attorney to reduce their sentences in exchange for their testimony. So Brown concluded that under those circumstances, the prisoners would testify to anything the prosecution might suggest. Once again, the court denied Brown's motion. Finally, Yavapai County officials hired two private attorneys to help prosecute the case.

Despite Brown's best efforts, the case against Smith proved too strong. The prosecution particularly focused on Smith's association with the other bandits before and after the robbery. The fact that a portion of the money stolen from the train was reportedly found on Smith certainly did not help his case. Following a one-day trial, Smith was found guilty and sentenced to thirty years' hard labor at the Yuma Territorial Prison.

Below is another newspaper article that appeared in the Arizona Weekly Journal-Miner on July 23, 1889, about the trip to Yuma from Prescott with the prisoners;

THE TRAIN ROBBERS

The Canyon Diablo Scoundrels
Safely Landed in the "Pen" at Yuma

"Sheriff Buckey O'Neill, of Yavapai County, along with his deputies, G. E. Brown and James Black, passed through here today on their way back to Prescott, having been to Yuma with the four noted Canyon Diablo Train Robbers, who were sentenced to twenty-five year sentences in the Territorial Penitentiary in Yuma, Arizona.

Deputy Sheriff Brown, who was seen at the Hollenbeck Train Station by express reporter, gave the following account of the trip and their experience with the prisoners:

'We started from Prescott, Arizona, on Saturday for Yuma in charge of the four Canyon Diablo Train Robbers who were 26 to 35 years old and as strong, handsome specimens of manhood as could be found anywhere.'

They appeared not to feel their position as at all hopeless until they were put on board the Southern Pacific cars at Colton, to which depot they were transferred from San Bernadino in hacks. Two of them had made an attempt to escape at Prescott Junction, but failed to get away.

It was quite evident, however, that they expected all the time on the trip, to make a successful break for liberty, for they were bright and cheerful throughout the trip until we reached Colton, not withstanding, that they were heavily ironed on the legs. At Colton they gave up all hope and became very despondent. They were in the same mood when they were left at Yuma.

> The men were all very tough customers and gave the sheriff and his deputies no end of trouble, as may be judged from the fact that they had to be kept in irons for six weeks.
>
> The law recently passed in Arizona making train robbery a capital offense would have been strictly applicable to these men, as their crime was committed after the passing of the act, but as it was held likely that they were not aware of the passage of the act, they were allowed to plead to alternative charge of highway robbery, which they did, and were sentenced to the above named term of years instead of being tried for train robbery, and probably hanged."

Although Smith along with his cohorts Halford, Stiren and Harvick started serving their sentences together at the Yuma Territorial Prison on November 24, 1889, the story of the Canyon Diablo bandits and lingering questions about Smith's guilt did not end there. Like many prisoners sentenced to Yuma, Smith contracted a respiratory infection (Tuberculosis). Four years into his stint, failing health motivated Smith to seek a pardon. The ensuing correspondence raises doubt that Smith actually participated in the robbery, and thus provides further evidence that the death penalty would have been wholly inappropriate in the case of the Canyon Diablo Robbery.

In a carefully crafted letter to Governor L. C. Hughes, Smith outlined the details of the events that transpired during the spring of 1889. At the center of Smith's request for clemency was his contention that he never participated in the robbery. On the date the crime occurred, Smith claimed that he was traveling to Hamilton, Nevada, where he hoped to continue the business of mining. Three days later, he claims he came upon Halford, Stiren, and Harvick at Wolf Crossing along the Little Colorado River about forty miles north of Canyon Diablo. He claimed to have briefly been acquainted with Halford and Harvick while working at an Arizona cattle ranch. At this point Smith claimed he had not heard news of the train robbery, and thus thought nothing of joining the men when he discovered they were all traveling in the same direction.

Rounded up by O'Neill's posse, Smith, with few Arizona friends and no money, disliked his chances of escaping punishment and made an impulsive decision to leap from the train carrying the prisoners to Prescott. Smith noted that no testimony was offered at his trial showing that he was at the scene of the robbery. After expending considerable effort and expenses to bring the three prisoners convicted in the Canyon Diablo heist to Prescott from Yuma, the prosecution had reversed course and decided to not let them testify when it learned that Halford, Stiren, and Harvick were prepared to swear under oath that Smith took no part in the robbery.

In their own letter to Governor Hughes that preceded Smith's clemency plea, Halford, Stiren and Harvick had essentially corroborated the details of the robbery and pursuit. When Hughes asked Prison Superintendent Thomas Gates to verify their claims, the warden had then forwarded Smith's request for a pardon along with his own letter vouching for Smith's exemplary behavior while in prison. Gates also noted that Smith was afflicted with rapid consumption, TB, and is likely to live but a short time. Smith received his pardon and was discharged from the Yuma Territorial Prison on August 13, 1893.

Below and on the next few pages the author presents several newspaper articles that appeared in the Phoenix Herald and the Arizona Weekly Journal-Miner regarding the sentencing of J. J. Smith and his early release from prison. The articles verify the information previously written by the author, and they also shed new information the question a lot of facts presented by Smith, his involvement in the train robbery and deepen the mystery of J. J. Smith's involvement in the Canyon Diablo Train Robbery.

In light of the development it appears plainly that Smith was in no way concerned in the robbery and the pardon was therefore issued. J. J. Smith, the bandit who, for his escape at Raton Pass, ended up with the longest prison sentence of the four convicted robbers, and actually served the shortest term, four years. Smith won his release from the Yuma Territorial Prison on August 13, 1893. Next to be freed was Dan Harvick, on December 25, 1896, after serving seven years of his 25-year sentence. John Halford and William Sterin received their releases on November 1, 1897, after serving eight years of their 25-year sentence. Halford is believed to have died in El Paso, Texas, of Tuberculosis, called *"The Prison Plague,"* a short time after his release from prison. There is no record on the later careers of J. J. Smith and Dan Harvick other than the following newspaper article that appeared in the Tucson Citizen on September 3, 1893, that shed more questions especially on Smith.

J. J. Smith Found on the Sonora Railroad

The consumptive train robber, J. J. Smith who was recently turned loose through the clemency of Governor Hughes, instead "of going home to die" like a good man, as the governor assured the public he would, went to Sonora, Mexico, where he now lives and to all appearances as strong and healthy a man as there is in that state. For a while he was lost to authorities but they finally located him in Guaymas, where he was living with a Mexican family in a secluded portion of the town.

When next seen he was at a railroad station in the Sonora Railroad in the act of taking notes on a locomotive. Possibly he was examining and admiring the beauty and complexity of its construction, but railroad men have a different opinion of his inquisitiveness and are reported to be watching him closely.

In Sonora he goes by the name of Shaw. It appeared J.J. Smith outsmarted the doctors in the Territorial Prison, gaining his full release serving again the shortest sentence of his companions.

Then on November 2, 1893, the Tucson Daily Star printed the following story that verified the fact that J. J. Smith's consumption, while his stay in prison, was nothing more than a well-planned and well played scam on prison officials as well as the Territorial Governor Hughes.

HE DRANK TO HIS HEALTH

Convict Smith Big Horn of Whiskey

Yet the Consumptive Is Still Alive
He Monkeyed with a buzz saw when he tackled the Commandant

"J. J. Smith, who was pardoned by Governor L. C. Hughes from the penitentiary for the reason (as alleged) of chronic consumption, has been again heard from. It has been discovered that William Sterin enlisted in the First U.S. Volunteer Cavalry Regiment, also called "Rough Riders," in the spring of 1898 under an assumed name. He was reputed to have been killed in the battle for San-Juan Hill on July 1, 1898.

It is also to be remembered that Smith was alleged (by the pardoning power of the Arizona Territorial Governor) to be on the verge of death, and that clemency was extended only on account of the fact that the poor devil wanted to go back east to die.

Of course it was rather odd that no one around the penitentiary knew that the fellow was nearly gone from consumption; only the sympathetic governor seemed aware of the gravity of his illness. Some of the people down in

Yuma were brutal enough to wonder what in the world the pardon was issued for, and scouted any idea but that Smith was as bale and hearty a man as was confined.

In the territorial hotel; but, of course, they could not be expected to have the ready and angelic sympathy of the territorial executive."

But Smith has again been heard of. No doubt he will continue to be heard of these many years to come. It seems that this gentleman with consumption and the uncommon cognomen went to Nogales after his release. Somehow the bracing climate of the border town was too robust for his delicate constitution, and so down he went to Magdelena, Sonora, Mexico.

Here he lived an idyllic sort of existence, looking frequently upon the odorous mescal and painting the town bright rosy carmine.

One dark day he met Federal Colonel Klosterlisky. The colonel was a delightful gentleman, in spite of his name, and so they had a drink together. Over their cups, Smith grew inquisitive and made inquiries of his companion as to the military and police commandant of the district, a certain Lieutenant Colonel Amelio.

Some of Colonel Amelio's police regulations were disapproved of by Smith and he made the remark that no one but the son of a dog would have passed such edicts.

As though in answer to having been observed, Smith's companion passed around the bar, and selecting a huge beer glass, poured it half full of fiery whiskey, then exclaimed, 'Holy Smoke! You're surely not going to take that sized jolt, are you? Oh no,' blandly replied his companion, 'I'm not going to drink it; never drink it; never that much myself. The fact of the matter is that you are the man who is going to drink the whiskey.' My esteemed friend, though generally known as Colonel Amelio, my name is Amelio Klosterlisky, Lieutenant Colonel in the Mexican Army.

You will leave the state of Sonora today, or I'll find employment for you in the mines. But first you will drink to my health." Smith was compelled to drink the full glass.

He then boarded the next train out of town, ran out of money and transportation to Calabasas, this side of the Arizona-Mexico border and was put off the train ten miles north of the station. He was left standing in the desert and has not heard from since."

Chapter Thirteen

Sheriff Buckey O'Neill totaled his expenses for the pursuit and capture of the Canyon Diablo Train Robbers, which he had paid out of his pocket, and came up with a figure of a little over $8,200 for the three week, two state, three-hundred-mile pursuit. He submitted the invoice for his expenses to the board of the Yavapai County Supervisors on July 9, 1889. After they considered the expense bill submitted, they agreed to pay $5,793.80 out of their General Fund, but they balked at the remainder, holding that O'Neill had far exceeded his jurisdiction and that the pursuit was well outside the Territory of Arizona, while happy with its successful conclusion, they felt it was not within the scope of Territorial reimbursement.

It must be noted that the Atlantic & Pacific Railroad sent the telegram to Sheriff O'Neill asking his help in the pursuit and capture of the outlaws. It was also understood they had previously agreed to pay for the expenses of the pursuit in lieu of being assessed a tax on the land they owned adjacent to the railroad tracks that ran through Yavapai County, as well as the agreement to pay the $4,000 reward that the A&P Railroad put up for the capture and the return of the outlaws and the money that was taken from the robbery. On July 10, 1889, an article appeared in the Arizona Weekly Journal-Miner Newspaper about Sheriff O'Neill's claim for the expenses from capturing and transporting the prisoners:

Sheriff Submits bill for Expense
Sheriff Buckey O'Neill's bill to the

> county called for payment of 16,000 miles which he said he and his posse traveled while out on the train robber business.
>
> The mildest expression that can be used in connection with the above is that it is misleading and is a misstatement of facts. The mileage bill put in by Sheriff O'Neill also included his three deputies, the transportation of the prisoners, as well as one or two trips to Lees Ferry to summon witnesses.
>
> The County Board of Supervisors has no right to be generous or liberal in the matter, and Sheriff O'Neill does not ask for either generosity or liberality from them, but for the simple payment of mileage due him and his deputies.

On July 10, 1889, the same day that Sheriff O'Neill received notice of the Board of Supervisors' decision, he wrote a letter *(reproduced below)* that was published in the Arizona Weekly Journal-Miner newspaper when the A & P railroad protested the decision of the Yavapai County Board of Supervisors;

> "In last evening's Weekly Journal-Miner newspaper appears a protest filed by the legal representatives of the Atlantic & Pacific Railroad against the valuation I have placed on the 350,000 acres of land selected and filed on by that company in this county, out of its grant of five and a quarter million acres owned in the county. While I do not care in what light the paid attorneys of the A&P Railroad may see fit to protest against

what I believe to be an honest and equitable assessment there is one portion of the protest in which they descend to false and untruthful statements against me personally that I desire to be corrected.

It is that portion which they state that the A&P Railroad has paid the expenses of pursuing and capturing the train robbers who committed crimes in this county. In the matter of the Canyon Diablo Robbers, so far from paying either of the men who were with me in that affair, or myself, thousands of dollars, the company deducted $2,500 out of the $4,000 reward it offered to pay expenses.

That is to say, that instead of $4,000 as it had promised, for the arrest and conviction of the four robbers and returning the $350,000 we recovered from the robbers that was considered by the A&P Railroad as an amount of no consequence, that it paid only $1,500, claiming the remaining $2,500 had been paid out by it for expenses.

So if anyone paid for the capture and conviction of the robbers, it was my deputies and I. In the matter of the assessment of the land; I think I have as much right and ability to estimate its' value per acre, although merely the representative of Yavapai County, as the men who earn their salaries by filling the positions of attorneys to foreign corporations."

Very respectfully,
William O. O'Neill, County Assessor.

On October 24, 1889, Sheriff O'Neill filed suit against the Board of the County of Yavapai in the Arizona Territory, for the balance of the expense money he felt was owed he and his deputies for the pursuit, capture and conviction of the Canyon Diablo Train Robbers. Herndon & Hawkins were appointed lawyers to assist the District Attorney in defense of the suit.

On Christmas Eve, 1889, the judge of the district court in Prescott delivered a summation that left no doubt where he stood. The judge's ruling follows;

> "Never did Roderick Dhu, winding his hunter's horn along the echoing shores of Loch Katrine, or Robin Hood in his largest sphere of freebooting, summon clans to more deadly than did the leader, J. J. Smith, with his gang of desperate highwaymen, upon fell purpose go.
>
> In an almost incredibly short time, Yavapai County's young sheriff O'Neill with his posse, in the saddle; and now commences that pursuit, which detailed by the evidence in this case, has scarcely a parallel for daring pertinacity in this or any other country.
>
> Across vast sandy plains, up and over rugged mesas and mountains, through canyons, gorges and mountain ranges, the pursuit waged, till at last the robbers are overtaken, a fight ensues, and the robbers are all captured. But it is over the Utah line; and it is contended for this reason, forsooth, the Sheriff can get nothing for his magnificent work."

On January 4, 1890, Sheriff O'Neill appealed the county courts decision to not pay him the balance of the funds due him for the pursuit and capture of the Canyon Diablo Train Robbers to the Arizona Superior Court and won his appeal.

Frustrated over the events that forced him to file suit against the county for his expense money in the pursuit and capture of the Canyon Diablo Train Robbers, Buckey O'Neill decided not to run for the office of sheriff when his term ran out. Instead he ran for office of Superior Court Judge and won the election. Curiously enough, though he did not know what fear was in the ordinary sense of the word, he was a very shy man. All his life he had to struggle against this as a politician.

One story told of him occurred soon after he was elected judge on January 15, 1891. A couple came before him to be married. The blushes of the bride were not to compare with those of the officiating officer. Somehow he got through the ceremony and pronounced them man and wife. The fair bride, however, seemed to think that the ceremony was incomplete and Buckey was in terror for fear it was necessary to kiss her. Eventually she retired with the groom, but no further than the outer office. A consultation was held and the lady returned, asking the judg;

"Haven't you forgotten something, sir?"

The judge picked the window from which he was ready to jump out of, but he was relieved of the situation when she added,

> "It seems to me that ring would look a heap better on my finger than in your vest pocket."

The excited judge fished out the ring he had forgotten and hastily restored it to the bride. Buckey was decisively routed only once and the victor on that occasion was an angry woman, her weapon an umbrella. It is on record that he adjourned court very hastily and left by way of the nearest window. Yet, though he was personally fearless, his nerve once failed him utterly.

On June 4, 1891, while still serving as a Superior Court Judge, Buckey O'Neill was appointed special agent to secure mining statistics of Yavapai County for the Eleventh Census. During these years in Prescott, Buckey O'Neill took part in everything in the community. He was a member of the Toughs Hose Company, a Prescott volunteer fire department. He also played baseball on a local traveling team. He was Adjutant General of the Arizona National Guard. He and Mrs. O'Neill, Pauline Schindler, were among the guests at various social functions, including weddings, and according to the custom of the times a list of wedding presents was published in the Arizona Weekly Journal-Miner, a local Prescott newspaper, with the names of the donors.

As gifts, the O'Neill's gave the bride and groom a set of silver tablespoons to the Duke-Foley wedding; and an antique plush rocker at the Sam Hill-Amy Dwyer wedding. Mrs. Pauline O'Neill was an active member of the Chautauqua Reading Club, and was frequently mentioned as giving a reading at meetings.

Buckey O'Neill ran for the office of Mayor of Prescott in 1897, and won the election, which was a fitting position, but when the Spanish-American War came along his patriotism got the best of him and he joined the U.S. Cavalry to go fight for our freedom.

Below is a picture of a political rally for Buckey O'Neill, who was running for the position of Mayor of the town of Prescott. Pauline O'Neill is in the front row wearing the white dress. Buckey O'Neill is in the back row in the middle with the black suit and white shirt. Buckey's brother Eugene O'Neill is sitting next to Pauline and behind her and is a dark suit with a white shirt. This photo was taken in 1897 and was found in our National Archives.

Chapter Fourteen

The balance of this story is dedicated to Buckey O'Neill and the part he played in the Spanish American War in Cuba. This part of the book will follow Buckey O'Neill's career in the Army with newspaper articles in chronological order to verify his career. The first article presented by the Author below appeared in the Prescott Courier newspaper on March 7, 1898. The article introduces Colonel A. O. Brodie as being commissioned by the Prescott City Council to recruit a volunteer cavalry regiment from Yavapai County to join Colonel Theodore Roosevelt, who was in charge of the U.S. Army in Cub;

COLONEL BRODIE OFFICIALLY ENDORSED

"The Prescott City Council, at its meeting last evening, did the proper thing in officially endorsing Colonel A. O. Brodie, who has applied for permission to raise a cavalry regiment in this territory in case of war with Spain. Colonel Brodie is eminently qualified for such a commission with his expletory military background. The following is a copy of an official letter authorized by the Prescott City Council to be sent to President McKinley:"

"To President McKinley, Washington D.C: Sir: We the Prescott City Council, Arizona Territory respectfully endorse Colonel A. O. Brodie of this city, for permission to recruit a cavalry regiment for active service should war be declared against Spain.

Colonel Brodie is a graduate of West Point, who has seen seven years of active service on the frontier as an officer of the first U.S. Army cavalry, in addition to commanding the First Regiment of the National Guard of Arizona.

He possesses to the highest degree the confidence and respect of the entire territory as a man and soldier of courage and ability. Sincerely urging that this request to recruit a regiment to represent Yavapai Territory in the field, be granted, we are, very respectfully,"

W. O. O'Neill, Mayor
B. H. Smith,
Gorham A. Bray,
W. W. Ross,

Territory of Arizona SS

I hereby certify that the signatures hereto attached are the signatures of the Mayor and Common Council of the City of Prescott.

Witness my hand and official seal of said city, this 7th day of March, 1898
(Seal) T.L. Schultz, City Clerk

On March 12, 1898, the article below was published in the Prescott Courier newspaper. It was regarding a notice from the U.S. Army in Washington, D.C., stressing that Colonel Brodie needed to step up the recruitment process as war is eminent;

OUR OWN SOLDIER BOYS

"Colonel A. O. Brodie has received instructions to hasten with all possible speed the organization of his cavalry battalion from Arizona and to precede with all haste to San Antonio, Texas, where the regiment will be organized; horses, uniforms and all accoutrements will be in waiting at the latter place. Instead of awaiting the arrival of a mustering officer from Washington Lieutenant Tupes, of the 15th Infantry, now stationed at Fort Whipple, has been instructed to muster in the battalion.

Preparations of quarters were commenced there today and Colonel Brodie expects to commence mustering in Volunteers tomorrow and hopes to be able to get away from here by Monday or Tuesday.

Governor McCord appointed James H. McClintock as captain of the troop which is being organized in the south. The captain of the troop form the north had not been designated at a late hour this afternoon although it is given out that Mayor Buckey O'Neill is an applicant for the position and that his brother Eugene Brady O'Neill is an applicant for one of the lieutenancy's.

Later, since the above was in type a special telegram has been received at this office announcing the appointment of Mayor O'Neill as captain of the troop from this section of the Territory. In addition to Eugene Brady O'Neill, it is stated also that Kean S. Charles, of Kingman, is an applicant of a lieutenant's commission."

Arizona was well represented in the war with Spain by two troop cavalries in what were crack regiments. Only the flower of Arizona will be on the flag they will carry into battle. The following telegram was received on April 25, 1898; by William Owen Buckey O'Neill showed the personnel of the officer's ranks, who will command the regiment.

> "All men desiring to enlist should apply at once to Buckey O'Neill in Prescott: Phoenix, A.T., April 25, 1898, William O. O'Neill, Prescott. Crack cavalry regiment to be raised in the west. Leonard Wood and Teddy Roosevelt go with it. Colonel A. O. Brodie to be one of the Majors.
>
> Arizona is to furnish 170 men. Go in and notify Apache County that its quote is six men; Coconino County, fourteen men; Mohave County, six men. Notify all that they must be able bodied; proper ages, between 18 and 45; good shots and good riders. Yavapai County's quota is 80 men. Get the best men you can enlist. Go to Fort Whipple as soon as possible. The officers leave Washington today for San Antonio, Texas."
>
> Alex O. Brodie, Colonel
> Commander of the Arizona Rough Riders

Mayor O'Neill received a telegram from Colonel Brodie the next day, April 26, 1898, that stated the western regiment would have distinctive uniforms. Kean St. Charles telegraphed that Mohave counties quota of men was ready. Johnny Francis wired from Flagstaff that Coconino County men were ready, with fourteen hot shots. Ten times as many as were taken are volunteering in Yavapai and much disappointment is expressed that so few men have been picked.

At this point after a lot of consideration, answering the call of patriotic duty, O'Neill decided to volunteer his service to his country. He realized he would have to tender his resignation as Mayor of Prescott and called an emergency meeting of the city council to announce his resignation and the reasons it needed to be done immediately.

On the morning of April 28, 1898, at the emergency city council meeting he called, Mayor O'Neill officially resigned from being mayor and along with his militia, joined the militia he had helped to raise for the U.S. Army, with the guarantee that he and his men would be kept together, through basic training and then guaranteed that they would also be together in battle as their own regiment.

This article appeared in the Prescott Courier paper on April 30, 1898, about O'Neill's resignation;

THE MAYOR RESIGNS

The City Council Passes Resolution to the Mayor's Patriotism

> "At a meeting of the city council held last evening, Mayor O'Neill tendered his resignation to the city council. The city council body took no action on it and will permit it to remain for probably a couple of months before taking action to see what the outcome of the war is as it is possible that

the mayor may return within that period. The council however passed the following resolutions last evening expressing their feeling toward their presiding officer:

Whereas; Our worthy mayor and president, who has so ably and acceptably presided over our council for the last year and a half, has felt it his duty to respond to the call of his country, and has expressed his willingness to surrender his life, if necessary, for the protection and maintenance of this nation; and, the following resolutions bearing upon the resignation of Mayor O'Neill to go to the front and fight for the Stars and Stripes:

Whereas; We deem it but a fitting tribute that this council express its appreciation of the services of Mayor O'Neill, not only to this body but also to the city; now, therefore, be ,

Resolved; That the loss of the services of Mayor O'Neill to the city at this time is much to be regretted from the absence of his ever-ready and wise aid, counsel and advices; however, we congratulate our Army in the acquisition of one so brave and true, and who has, as we believe made this sacrifice for no other purpose or motive than that which is prompted by duty and patriotism; and be it further,

Resolved; That these resolutions be spread at length upon the minutes of the council, a copy of the city, and an engrossed copy presented to President O'Neill.

The city council will present Mayor O'Neill a six shooter with which the Courier hopes he will have a chance to slay old Weyler, himself."

Below is a photo of the Rough Rider volunteers marching down Montezuma street to be sworn in Courtesy of Sharlot Hall Museum. MIL218PD

One week passed from the time Mayor O'Neill resigned his post, and after working with his regiment so that they knew how to march, salute and form, they loaded all of their horses and supplies. Then they met at the Courthouse Square for a going away party. Below is an article that appeared in the Prescott Courier newspaper on May 8, 1898, about the celebration and the city, county and state's farewell.

AN OUTBURST OF PATRIOTISM

The citizens of Prescott turn out by the Hundreds to Bid their Soldiers Farewell

The greatest Demonstration Ever witnessed in this Mountain City

"Prescott has achieved quite a reputation for her enthusiasm the departure of the Arizona on occasions, and for her hospitality, but all previous records were broken by her citizens Wednesday afternoon on the departure of the Arizona volunteers for the cowboy regiment at San Antonio, Texas.

The entire town seemed to be on the streets, in the plaza and at the depot to see the brave boys off, and the remark was frequently heard that it was not known where they all came from.

At four o'clock the volunteers arrived from Fort Whipple, preceded by the Prescott Brass Band, and were ranged in line in front of the band stand in the plaza, from which Governor McCord delivered his address in delivering the national colors to the troop from Phoenix, a synopsis of which appeared in the last issue of this paper. The governor was repeatedly applauded during the delivery of his address, and his remarks showed that he was inspired by the spirit of the occasion, and was possessed of most patriotic sentiments.

Honorable H. E. Morrison acted as chairman of the gathering, and announced the program and introduced the speakers. After the flag had been presented by Governor McCord, and on behalf of the soldiers, accepted by Colonel A. O. Brodie, the commissions from Governor McCord were presented to the officers by Adjutant General Lewis. Captain J. H. McClintock responded on behalf of the officers.

Reese M. Ling, city attorney, then presented to Captain O'Neill a handsome six shooter and scabbard, a present from the members of the city council. Captain O'Neill responded in a few brief and appropriate remarks.

Colonel J. F. Wilson and T. G. Norris each delivered short, patriotic addresses, and a glee club from the Phoenix volunteers sang a patriotic song. The exercises were interspersed throughout with music from the band.

During the ceremony Captain James McClintock was presented an Arizona and American flag that was made by the wives of the volunteers from Phoenix. The flag had an interesting history. The flag was made with ribbons instead of cords and thus could be distinguished at some distance from other flags.

Chairman Morris, at the conclusion of the ceremony, presented a young mountain lion from Bob Brow to the volunteers as a mascot. During the progress of ceremony an enthusiastic, patriotic citizen in the crowd, proposed three-cheers for President William McKinley, which was enthusiastically responded to by all present.

The march to the train depot was made in the following order: Prescott Brass Band; Grand Army veterans; The Prescott Fire Department; Governor McCord and his staff; the Prescott School children; and then followed up by the citizens present at the ceremony.

At the train depot hand shaking, farewells and tears were the order until the train pulled out of the station, some of the partings being pathetic.

The train, consisted of four passenger coaches and one combination care, was beautifully decorated with streamers of red, white and blue along with banners with appropriate inscriptions along their sides. The run to Albuquerque will be made in these cars without change.

The combination car was filled to overflowing with edibles for the use on the trip. A sum of $600 was raised by subscription yesterday within a few hours, with which these supplies were purchased. A large number of hams were purchased and boiled. Also a lot of fresh mutton, a barrel of pigs-feet, pickles by the case, canned fruit of all kinds, a card load or so of bread, and other things too numerous to mention, was included in the list; while as luxuries there were 300 corn cob pipes, several caddies of tobacco and three barrels of bottled beer.

The train was in charge of Conductor, F. Beam; Engineer, Dan Grilles at the throttle; and Fireman, J. Latly, in the cab with him was General Passenger Agent G.M. Sargent, in private car 98, and went with the boys to see them safely turned over to the Santa Fe Pacific Railroad when they arrive at Albuquerque, New Mexico. Simon J. Murphy and his son, H. W. Murphy, also accompanying him.

While the train was scheduled to leave Prescott at 6 o'clock it was not until 7:15 before it finally pulled out of the train depot. Engineer Gilles pulled the train out very slowly until the train had passed *through the cut in the yards, while a perfect sea of handkerchiefs and parasols were waved in the air and a chorus of shouts went up from hundreds of voices.*

As the train was about to depart, the volunteers expressed themselves as being overwhelmed with the rousing farewell demonstration accorded them by the towns people, and said it would forever have remembered by them wherever the fate of war might carry them.

A railroad postcard of the Prescott Train Depot as it appeared from 1887 to 1986. The last passenger train rolled out of the station in 1978. Tracks were removed permanently in 1986 ending train service to downtown Prescott, Arizona.

Chapter Fifteen

The old war spirit was revived in the hearts of the veterans of the war of this rebellion, and those of both sides turned out in force to emphasize the cordial farewell tendered to the young volunteers.

A Cuban flag was carried in the procession by Major John Reese, of Barret Post, G.A.R. Judge J. D. Bethune, an ex-artillery captain of the confederate army and Colonel J. F. Wilson, also an ex-confederate officer, acted as color guards to it. John Crellin, an ex-union soldier, was the standard bearer of our national colors in the procession, while George Augustine and John Curtin were color guards to it.

Below and on the next page is a newspaper article that appeared in the Phoenix Herald on May 3, 1898, about the Special Arizona Flag the troops would be carrying into battle.

PHOENIX WOMEN MAKE FLAG

> "The Arizona made flag has an interesting history. It has ribbons instead of cords and thus could be distinguished at some distance from other flags. It was carried by the Arizona troops to Cuba and was the first unfurled on Cuban soil. Sergeant Wright of Yuma and others carried it up the hill and planted it in plain sight of the disembarking troops. When Captain McClintock told the Arizona men that it was their flag, a great shout went up and shots were fired from their revolvers that gave the Arizona

> emblem a noisy salute. Then the battleships took notice and fired the customary formal salute with guns. Thus the flag made by devoted women in Phoenix became conspicuous in the nation's eye and became a trophy sacred for all it symbolized.
>
> The flag was carried in the charge up San-Juan Hill and was cut by a number of bullets. After the Cuban War it was brought back to Phoenix and is now carefully kept in the governor's office. In 1911, when Theodore Roosevelt came to Phoenix for the dedication of Roosevelt Dam, he was presented a piece of cloth of which the flag was made that he might have a souvenir of the American flag made in Arizona., which led his Rough Riders to victory in their desperate charge against the Spanish entrenchments on the out-skirts of Santiago De Cuba."

The two Arizona regiments arrived by train in Albuquerque at noon on May 9, 1898. They boarded the next train that took them from Albuquerque to San Antonio, Texas, where they were to head to the Army Fort where they were to train and await further orders. They arrived at San Antonio late in the afternoon of May 11, 1898. Upon arrival the officials there confirmed the following roster of Troop B: Captain William Owen Buckey O'Neill, First Lt., Frank Frantz; Second Lt, J. B. Patterson. And the following members that made up the balance of Troop B: Daniel L. Hogan, John L. Howard, Frank M. McCarty, Bruce C. Bartos, Edward Nelson, Edward Liggett, Robert M.

Hicks, Fred W. Bugbee, William F. Wallace, William H. Danforth, Charles A. Scharf, Henry W. Nash, John W. Jackson, George A. McCarty, King O. Healey, George Kasrens, Harry P. Gibbons (who the author met in 1968, as a neighbor in our apartment complex, and who displayed the carbine he used in the Spanish American War over his fireplace. He also shared his photo album and talked about the war with me on many occasions. Harry was a very interesting man.), Floyd J. Bradshaw, Henry P. Byrnes, Pilonde O. Reynolds, Lewis Doherty, George H. wells, Henry J. Page, William Wallace, Walter D. Shaw, James A. Barthel, Peter K. Tuttle, Arthur L. Pettit, Lous P. Paxton, Frank Klingman, Adam H. May, James A. Jackson, Cade C. Griffin, William W. Marine, Rufus H. French, Wilbur D. Somers, Fred B. Webb, Anthony D. Randebaugh, J. D. Johnson, John W. Dell, Henry Greenley, Jason T. Howland, Henry Wamtoych, Frank L. Jackson, Charles Assay, William Shackleford, M. S. Azbil, John Casi, Emile Sheenaker, John Fox, H. B. Frantz, Frank Waller, J. H. Hanson, William Holtzeschue, Carl Greenwald, Samuel Greenwood, W. W. Morgan, T. L. Sullivan, P. J. Trowbridge, Lawrence Rogerer, John Hamilton, Thomas Youst, J. G. Rupert, C. W. McAndrews, John Harner, F. J. Garrett, Samuel H. Younger and Charles L. Danforth.

Prescott Courier article, May 16, 1898, verifies the fact that the Arizona Regiment arrived in San Antonio and were about to depart for Tampa, Florida. From there they would be deployed to Cuba;

Arizona Regiments on to Cuba

Arizona Volunteers Leave next Saturday

"Two telegrams were received Saturday by Governor McCord from the Arizona Cavalry Volunteers in rendezvous at San Antonio. The first was from Major Brodie, Stating that the Arizona troops were the first to fill the muster and rendezvous and that it is expected that the command will leave for Cuba next Saturday.

Another telegram was received from Captain McClintock, stating that the Arizona regiments having arrived at San Antonio would be the first on the ground and were pronounced by Colonel Wood to be the finest body of men he has ever seen. Captain McClintock also stated the troops will march next week."

"The Arizona officers are endeavoring to get the Secretary of War to date their commissions from the time they were commissioned by Governor McCord. Major Brodie's commission, if this is done, will date from April 25, 1898, and Captains O'Neill's and McClintock's from April 28, 1898. Governor McCord on Saturday wired the request to the authorities in Washington."

Mrs. Pauline O'Neill kindly allowed the Arizona Journal-Miner newspaper to print a letter she received from her husband, Captain O'Neill, on June 1, 1898, while he was with his regiment in Tallahassee, Florida, while on the road to Tampa, Florida;

"The men received an enthusiastic reception all along the railroad line, *proving conclusively that the north and south were united as one great people.*

The boys gave away all of their hard tack to the young ladies along the road, and, in consequence, were short on rations.

Arizona has the honor of carrying the only stand of colors that was presented to the regiment by W. R. Clayton, of Phoenix; in fact, Arizona has the honor of outfitting the entire regiment with mascots in the shape of the lion and some dogs. We expect to reach Tampa June 2, 1898, and will probably go to Cuba or Santiago with the fifth consignment. The boys wish to be remembered by all their Arizona friends."

The photo above of the Rough Rider Camp in Tampa, Florida, was found in the Florida State Historical Archives

The two Arizona regiments spent the next two weeks training and getting ready to head to Cuba. They received their orders to meet Colonel Roosevelt and his troops in Tampa, Florida, so they could all board ships and head to Cuba. The following article appeared in the Prescott Courier on June 5, 1898;

ARIZONA BOYS AT TAMPA

"The Arizona regiments have arrived in Tampa, Florida, Sunday night and are awaiting orders to embark for Cuba. The article went on to say that the 750 to 800 horses that will be needed for the regiments will be brought to San Antonio and various other points in the west. Captains Earl D. Thomas and Howell S. Bishop of the Fifth Cavalry have been detailed by the Secretary of War to proceed to the following points to buy horses and ship them immediately to Tampa, Florida, to be transported with the troops to Cuba: Prescott, Arizona; Santa Fe, New Mexico; Muskoegee, Illinois; and Guthrie, Oklahoma."

The photo on the previous page is courtesy of Sharlot Hall Museum that was taken of Captain "Buckey" O'Neill at the Roughrider Camp at Tampa, Florida. PO1117P

The two weeks the Arizona regiments spent in Tampa were a challenge to say the least. While brief, it presented a panoramic view of the logistical incompetence that characterized the Cuban operation of the Spanish-American War. The town itself lay on pine-covered flats at the end of a one-track railroad line, a miserable collection of shanties, saw grass and sand dunes infested with clouds of bloodthirsty mosquitoes and armies of spiders and centipedes. In contrasting splendor, the thirteen minarets of the Tampa Bay Hotel stood in the distanced. This bizarre structure, covering six acres and containing 500 rooms on five floors, became the principal gathering place for Army officers and newspapermen; sipping on mint julips and waving aside the 110-degree heat and humid, fetid air with palm leaf fans on the great balconies. Colonel Roosevelt's friend, the dashing correspondent and creative writer, Richard Harding Davis, referred to the Tampa Bay Hotel lounging as *"the rocking chair period of the war."*

Since the hotel contained a fine gambling casino, Captain O'Neill spent most of his time at the casino. But few such pleasures could lessen the scene of utter chaos in Tampa when the Rough Riders arrived to join the regulars of Shafter's V Corps. The single track railroad was so overtaxed that freight cars loaded with provisions, medicines, and material were backed up for miles. Three hundred cars loaded with war supplies were stalled along the track.

Rough Rider officers pictured in front of the Tampa Bay Hotel, this picture was found in the Florida State Archives, circa 1898

Invoices and bills of lading were misplaced in the confusion, and the Army had to break the seals on the cars to ascertain what they carried. Another day, fifteen cars loaded with lightweight uniforms were side tracked twenty-five miles from Tampa, while troops suffered in the intense humidity and heat, wearing insufferable winter woolens. The stench of rotting meat in the stalled cars attracted dense swarms of green bottle flies; the palmetto overgrown sand dunes were littered with a bedlam of tents, piled packing crates, horse and mule remudas and attendant saddles, harness and forage; and on every point of the compass were thirty-thousand drilling, milling soldiers, plus stevedores, newspapermen, government officials, camp followers, civilian gawkers, visitors, well-wishers, old soldiers, handshaking politicians, ladies, ship captains, sailors, and school children. Not in this world or the next, a Chicago reporter proclaimed as the men and horses boarded the ships to set sail for the final leg of their voyage to Cuba;

> "shall I ever see the equal of the mess at the Tampa ship docks. I have never seen sights at dock and railhead that were unmatched, except in some huge lunatic asylum."

One New York recruit expressed his disgust with the place telling an eager reporter that on his first day in camp he had been bitten by mosquitoes, stung by a tarantula, felt a touch of malaria, ran his bayonet into his hand, sat on an ant bed, stepped on an alligator, found a snake in his boot, and felt *"like a dirty duce in a new deck of cards."*

Mrs. Pauline O'Neill received a short telegram the next day, June 7, 1898, that she also shared with the Arizona Weekly Journal-Miner and it stated;

> "I am writing from Key West, Florida. Companies K and L received orders today to go to Cuba today. Our Company A is the only regiment under those direct orders."

Captain Buckey O'Neill and his men, along with their horses, boarded the transport ship later that week in route to Cuba to join Colonel Roosevelt to begin the Cuban operation. The telegram shows the grit and bravery of Captain O'Neill.

The next report that was received on the progress of the Arizona regiments came by way of a telegram from the War Department on June 24, 1898, that was forwarded to the Prescott Courier and it read as follows;

> "A dispatch from Port Au Prince, Haiti, dated June 24, states that there were two casualties during the landing of troops at Baiquiri, Cuba. A corporal and Private English, of Troop D, 10th Cavalry, a colored regiment, fell between the ship and the pier while disembarking from the ship. Captain Buckey O'Neill plunged into the sea at the risk of his own life, but the men were crushed before he reached them. O'Neill the former sheriff and mayor of Prescott, the Arizona Territory."

A picture of the Rough Riders at the docks, when they landed in Cuba. This photo was found in the Florida State National Archives

Chapter Sixteen

There were no more reports or letters sent to Pauline O'Neill explaining what happened from the time Captain O'Neill landed in Cuba until July 2, 1898. That is really no surprise though. The troops were either in battle or marching toward the battle with the entrenched Spanish Army who occupied Cuba at that time. The following sad report was sent to the War Department and a copy was forwarded to the Prescott Courier from Mrs. Pauline O'Neill:

> "Saboney, Cuba, July 2, 1898, - "The American loss in the first day of battle was heavier than was expected. It is, even yet, too early to estimate the number that were killed or wounded. The Cubans suffered more casualties, in proportion, than the Americans; Captain William Owen Buckey O'Neill of the Rough Riders, was killed; Sergeants Hallets and Burrows were wounded.
>
> The most glorious achievement of the day was the charge, up San-Juan Hill, by the cowboys with the rain of Spanish shells pouring down upon them. But they never wavered. The men acted well on every side, but the Rough Riders, with the 71st New York and the 10th Cavalry, swept everything before them, capturing San-Juan Hill, held by a thousand Spaniards, and three block houses, defended by their artillery."

Private dispatches were received in Prescott yesterday from Washington, D.C. stating that there was no official news of the death of Captain O'Neill, which gives an already mourning town, section and territory a ray of hope that the gallant soldier, the intrepid leader, both in war and peace, both in the political arena and on the battlefield, may still be alive and again come home to greet his loving wife and his hosts of friend all over this land to take his place once more as one of the most public spirited, patriotic, progressive and popular citizens of Arizona. Let us all hope that the sad news may prove a mistake and that we will once more feel the magnetic grasp of the hand of our noble friend. Immediately upon the spreading of the report of the death of Captain Buckey O'Neill, every flag in the city was lowered to half-mast and telegrams flashed over the wires for more particulars and a confirmation of the news, while telegrams of condolence were received in Prescott. It has been said that the pen is mightier than the sword. In Arizona, Captain Buckey O'Neill had no peer in the use of the pen, and when duty called he laid that pen aside for the sword, and we all pray that he may wield it as long and as invincibly as he has the pen;

> "Washington, D.C., July 3, 1898: Mrs. W. O. O'Neill was tonight officially notified that her late husband William Owen "Buckey' O'Neill was killed in action at San-Juan Hill, Cuba."

Later that same day, July 3, 1898, Pauline Schindler O'Neill received a confirming private dispatch from the U. S. War Department confirming the devastating news;

> *"Washington, D.C., July 3, 1898: Mrs. W. O. O'Neill was tonight officially notified that her late husband William Owen "Buckey" O'Neill was killed in action at San-Juan Hill, Cuba."*

This, indeed, dispels the one ray of hope which was held to the last. The Arizona Weekly Journal-Miner quotes;

> *"We shall see our gallant friend no more. Arizona has lost one of her brightest and most useful citizens and his country a most gallant soldier who, had death spared him, would have surely made his mark in military as he has civil affairs; but, even in death, he has covered himself with a glory which few men can live and achieve. Let us honor his memory which few men can live and achieve."*

Ironically, one of the Canyon Diablo Train Robbers, William Sterin, after his release from prison enlisted in the First U.S Volunteer Cavalry Regiment, AKA the "Rough Riders," under Captain Jim McClintock in the spring of 1898. He registered under a different name so that he would not be recognized by Captain O'Neill. He was reportedly one of the first men killed in the battle at San-Juan Hill early in the morning of July 1, 1898, the first day of action.

A later report was sent to the Prescott Courier the next day which was the Fourth of July, 1898, and followed up how Captain O'Neill lost his life and it reads as follows;

"Captain O'Neill was standing above the trenches just in front of his men, talking with Captain Howse of the artillery. Spattering bullets were striking all around him, and one of his sergeants along with some of his other troops anxiously asked him to take cover in the trenches.

Captain O'Neill's answer was, Sgt., the Spanish bullet isn't made that can kill me. Thus spoke the gallant Captain at the head of his troops at the foot of San-Juan Hill before the battle of Santiago. The Rough Riders already had begun their movement up the hill toward the Spanish entrenchments on San-Juan Hill and the greatest land battle of the Spanish-American War was beginning. Captain O'Neill's troops gathered from various parts of Arizona were lying down and seeking shelter from a hail of Spanish bullets, awaiting the order from their commander to move forward.

Their captain, Buckey O'Neill, was standing upright before them, smoking a cigar and walking up and down the line. He was an idol of the Arizona Rough Riders and many of them continued to call for him to lie down to save himself.

As he answered the sergeant, who asked him to lay down, he was laughing and while the smile was still on his face, he crumpled up and pitched forward. A Spanish bullet went through his jaw and came out of his neck. He died instantly before his body reached the ground."

Captain Buckey O'Neill's body was buried where it fell, but after the battle of San-Juan Hill was finally over, his body was later removed and placed in Arlington National Cemetery in Washington, D.C. Theodore Roosevelt, the Commander and chief of the Rough Riders in Cuba, wrote about the death of Captain Buckey O'Neill in his official military report;

"The most serious loss that I and the regiment could have suffered befell just before we charged up San-Juan Hill. Captain O'Neill was strolling up and down in front of his men, smoking his cigarette, for he was inveterately addicted to the habit.

He had a theory which was, of course, wrong, though in a volunteer organization the officers should certainly expose themselves very fully, simply for the effect of the men; our regimental toast on the transport running, the officers; may the war last until each is killed, wounded or promoted.

As the captain moved to and fro, his men begged him to lie down, and one of his sergeants said, 'Captain, a bullet is sure to hit you.' O'Neill took his cigarette out of his mouth, and blowing out a cloud of smoke, laughed and said, 'Sergeant, the Spanish bullet isn't made that will kill me.'

A little later he discussed for a moment with one of the regular officers the direction from which the Spanish fire was coming. As he turned on his heel a bullet struck him in the mouth and came out at the back of his head; so that even before he fell his wild and gallant soul had gone into darkness."

Below is a photo found in our National Archives of Colonel Teddy Roosevelt, standing in the middle next to the flag with the suspenders, on top of San Juan Hill after the battle with his Roughriders.

On the following pages is an article that appeared in the Prescott Courier on July 6, 1898, confirming the men killed, wounded or still missing in action from the Arizona Roughrider brigade in the Spanish-American War;

THE DEAD AND WOUNDED

"Arizona thrills with admiration and pride over the victories, deeds and sacrifices her sons are enacting in defense of our nation. Their glorious names are echoing throughout the nation, but amid her joys, sorrow forever fallen heroes tinge the occasion with sadness. On the scarred field of battle some of her bravest and dearest sons have paid the last libations that liberty calls. Among the number the gallant Captain W. O. Buckey O'Neill, whose name is on the lips of all, a great leader, a true friend, and a man of unequalled indomitable will and determination. His name will add luster to the roll of patriotic heroes who will adorn our country's historic page."

THE FIRST FULL and AUTHENTIC LIST of the CASUALTIES in CAPTAIN O'NEILL'S company

"The Journal-Miner is indebted to First Sergeant W. W. Greenwood, of A Troop, Rough Riders, for the following which is a correct list of the killed and wounded of that troop, and which is the first full and authentic list yet published."

KILLED

"Colonel Charles A. Witkoff, Twenty Second Infantry; Lieutenant Colonel John M. Hamilton, Ninth Cavalry; Captain W. O. Buckey O'Neill, First Volunteer Cavalry; Lieutenant W. H. Smith, Tenth Cavalry; Major Forse, First Cavalry; Lieutenant Michie, Son of Professor Michie; Lieutenant Jules G. Ord, Sixth Infantry; Lieutenant William E. Shipp, Tenth Cavalry; Corporal George Dougherty; Private James Boyle; Private Stanley Hollister; Private Louis Reynolds; Private Ed Liggett; Lieutenant Fred Champlin; Corporal J. K. Hall; Private C. B. Perry; Sergeant H. H. Haywood; Private Miley Hendricks; Private William Soutz; Private John Swetman; Private Oliver Norton; Private David Logue; Private Roy V.

Cashiu, Private Henry C. Greene; and Private John F. Robinson."

MISSING IN ACTION

Corporal D. Cussin and Trumpeter James Cork."

WOUNDED

"Lieutenant Colonel John H. Patterson, Twenty Second Infantry; Lieutenant Colonel Henry Carrol, Commanding First Brigade Cavalry Division; Major Henry S. W. Wessells, Third Cavalry; Captain Augustus P. Blockson, Sixth Cavalry; Captain John Dorr, Sixth Cavalry; Captain George K. Hunter, Third Cavalry; Captain George A. Dodd, Third Cavalry; Captain Charles W. Taylor, Ninth Cavalry; Lieutenant Frank R. McCoy, Tenth Cavalry; Lieutenant Winthrop, Ninth Cavalry; Adjutant S. W. Wood, Ninth Cavalry; Lieutenant Haskell, First Volunteer Cavalry; Lieutenant Joseph A. Carr; Cadet Lieutenant William Haskell; Second Lieutenants David J. Leahy, H.K Deveraux and First Lieutenant R. C. Day, Lieutenant A. L. Mills, First Cavalry; Lieutenant Orria B. Meyer, Third Cavalry; Lieutenant Arthur Thaver, Third Cavalry; Captain John Broadman, Tenth Infantry; First Sergeant W. W. Greenwood; Sergeants James Greenly, Stephen Pate, Dan Hughes, Jerry Lee, Fred C. Wesley, Timothy Breene, Fred C. Meyers, H. H. Haywood, Walter Cash, John G. Adams, David Robinson, William J. Greenly, Corporal H. White;

Trumpeter Emil Cassi; Keene D. Robinson, William G. Simmons, Joseph G. Kline, W. W. Carpenter, D. M. Bell, W. R. Reber, Basil Ricketts, Corporals Harp White, Henry Meagher, Herman W. Wynkoop, John Mullen, James Dean, Edwin C. Waller, Morgan Powers, William Freeman, Sam Goldberg, A. F. Perry, B. G. Davis, J. J. Rogers, J. W. Davis, George Seaver; Privates H. J. Waller, C. B. Jackson, Ed O'Brien, Fred W. Bugber, Stanley Hollister, Han Smith; Last name only Murphy, Han, Smith, Hammer, Starr. M. Wetmore, Trumpeter; William Bailey, Warren E. Crockett, Thomas M. Holmes, Ed W. Johnson, F. W. Miller, R. L. McMillern, G. W. Detamore, John P. Hall, Otto Menger, C. E. McKinley, J. W. McGregor, H. M. Gibbs, J. G. Winter, R. C. Clark, Winslow Clark, Louis Goer, Alvin C. Ash, John McSperran, Benjamin Long, William Sadler, Mason Mitchell, A. E. Scoby, F. R. McDonald, Trumpeter; G. R. Eugart, Dick Oskinsom, O. E. Parker, B. V. Thompson and Dave Warford, along with J. H. Waller; Fred Bugbee; and C. B. Jackson all received ugly wounds. They had their wounds dressed back at the division hospital and then went back to their perspective companies and took their places on the firing line. C. B. Perry was shot through the head but will live."

"Quartermaster Sergeant George Walsh and Alexander H. Wallace died of fever. The latter joined the troop at

> San Antonio and will be well remembered by the miners of this section, as his vocation was that of mining. Sergeant Greenwood gives a very graphic description of events after their landing in Cuba as he was standing within arms-length of Captain "Buckey" O'Neill when that brave officer fell. Sergeant Greenwood was shot in two places, one ball striking him in the instep passing through the foot and coming out through his heel on the sole of his foot. The other ball struck his leg just below the knee.

The reason that I have listed all of these names is very simple. I believe it is important for the reader to know that these folks were real people who gave their lives or were injured in the line of duty protecting our liberty and freedom. It is also being respectful to families' who members served in the Spanish-American War.

The following is another newspaper article that appeared in the Prescott Courier and the Phoenix Herald. Some of the facts are repeated, but there are some interesting facts relating to Mrs. Pauline O'Neill when she first found out about the death of her husband, William Owen Buckey O'Neill.

OUR BRAVE DEAD

> "The community was thrown into the most profound sadness and gloom on Saturday night by the receipt of the news that Captain W. O. Buckey O'Neill of Prescott's "Rough Riders" had fallen in Friday's battle. The

telegram came about 10 o'clock and the news spread like a wildfire. Expressions of the deepest sorrow were heard from the lips of everyone, and hope although it was against hope was felt that it might prove a mistake. Later, however, telegrams were received confirming the sad news.

Mrs. Pauline O'Neill had been in Phoenix for several days attending to her husband's business, when the news was flashed over the wires she was on the train speeding homeward, all unconscious of the overwhelming sorrow which awaited her upon her arrival back in Prescott. Father Queta secured a carriage and met her at the train depot to impart the news to her, and the fact of this meeting her instinctively told her that something had happened to her loved one. Immediately upon his speaking to her and being told that a carriage was waiting, she inquired; "Has anything happened to Owen?" Father Queta told her there was bad news concerning him and she broke completely down, her grief over her loss being inconsolable."

Chapter Seventeen

The death of Captain O'Neill was characteristic of the individual. In private life he was brilliant, impulsive and dashing. He never counted the cost of anything he undertook. With him the impulse to do a thing was to attempt to accomplish it and the attempt was accompanied by all the energy and spirit at his command. He was born a leader of men and his impetuous daring to attempt what others shrank from won for him the admiration of even his enemies. When General Lawton ordered an advance to be made upon the enemies' position, Captain O'Neill was the first to respond. With the ever uppermost impulse in his mid "to do or die," he led the charge, and the telegrams state that he had not proceeded over twenty yards until he fell forward dead, pierced by a Spanish bullet. It was a heroic end of a brave and fearless man.

On that memorable Fourth of July, Arizona Territorial Governor McCord, representing all the people in territory sent the following telegram of condolence to the bereaved widow, a man whom we shall see no more, but whose deeds never die:

Mrs. William Owen O'Neill,

"It is with great sorrow that I learned of your husband's death. He died bravely leading his men in defense of his country. He died with his face to the foe that his country might live. Every loyal heart in Arizona sends out to you its deepest sympathy. All Arizona mourns his death."

Myron H. McCord
Governor of Arizona

Even in death Captain Buckey O'Neill showed his great respect and his responsibility to his wife, Pauline. She received $200,000 from the proceeds of a life insurance policy he had taken out on his life. $200,000 in 1898 would have equated to a buying power today of over 3 million dollars, taking into account inflation. She was set for life because Buckey was an intelligent and responsible husband. On August 7, 1898, the following article was nationally published by the San Francisco Examiner, along with the Phoenix Republican and the Prescott Courier newspapers;

The official U.S Army Report on the Death of Captain O'Neill
September 18, 1898
Captain "Buckey" O'Neill

How the Mayor and Rough Riders died

"The late Captain O'Neill, Troop A, First United States Volunteer Cavalry, was one of the most striking among the many odd characters from all walks of life who made up the famous regiment of Rough Riders. A plainsman, legislator, a notorious gambler, an able economist, a man devoid of fear, he earned a distinction in the combination of traits which may be said none of his comrades reached. The account of his death was related the other day by a member of his troop who passed through Long Island City on his way to the south after being mustered out.

He was William Pulsing, a German-American business man of New Orleans, who was accepted into the regiment largely on account of his regular Army experience. Mr. Pulsing was found at the Red Cross Hospital at Long Island City, where he was staying overnight, though little worse from his campaign experiences; Buckey O'Neill, he said, 'won his nickname from the fact that he was always given to bucking the tiger' every gambling game in site. He was noted through a large part of the west for his gambling propensities.

Troop A, of which he was Captain, was not engaged at El Caney, but they took part in the general advance on Santiago. He lost his life at the Battle of San-Juan Hill. The troop was deployed along a creek, and the firing was hot. I asked Captain O'Neill if he would allow me to go ahead and reconnoiter. And on receiving permission, I started out and ran into a road a short distance ahead, which had been sunk by the use of troops and wagons, about a foot below the surrounding soil. I reported to Captain O'Neill that this would be a good place for the troop to find temporary shelter and we all went forward. The members of the troop lay down on this road.

The Mouser bullets were whizzing rapidly over us, but Captain O'Neill, who was always accustomed to expose himself recklessly to fire, stood upright, apparently unconscious of the danger. He was talking to an adjutant General, though who the general was I do not know. Suddenly a Mouser bullet struck him squarely in the mouth, going in so *evenly that his teeth were not injured. He fell to the ground at once. I and a man named Boyle, who was afterward killed in battle, picked him up and carried his body to the rear. He died their seconds later.*

Captain O'Neill was noted for his writings on political economy besides his gambling tendencies. He was the Mayor of Prescott, Arizona, when he enlisted, and was the first man to introduce the theories of Henry George into that town."

On the following page is a very interesting newspaper article that appeared in the Prescott Courier along with the Phoenix Republican on May 18, 1901. It shares some interesting information regarding "Buckey" O'Neill's widow, after a long engagement to, and her marriage to "Buckey" O'Neill's younger brother, Eugene O'Neill:

CAPTAIN O'NEILL'S WIDOW WEDS

Bridegroom is the young brother of "Buckey" O'Neill

"Phoenix, May 18, 1901, Eugene Brady O'Neill and Mrs. Pauline O'Neill were married this afternoon at Sacred Heart Church by Reverend Father Novadus of the Roman Catholic Diocese of Tucson. The bridegroom is a brother and the bride was the widow of the late W. O. O'Neill, better known as Captain 'Buckey' O'Neill of B Company, Teddy Roosevelt's Rough Riders, and was one of the first to fall on the historic battlefield of San-Juan Hill, Cuba.

> Mrs. O'Neill is a large property owner in Phoenix and is a very talented woman. From time to time her library work has been given premieres in 'The Examiner.' Her husband is a younger brother of her former husband and is a well-known local practicing attorney."

After marrying Buckey O'Neill's brother, Eugene, she and her husband sold all of their business and land holdings in Prescott and moved permanently to Phoenix; where the couple lived until her death in 1961 at the age of 96. She outlived her second husband, Eugene, but she kept busy after his death involved in many charitable endeavors and handling the family finances.

Pauline O'Neill has too often been hidden in the shadows of her famous husband. Like Buckey though, she was ambitious, bright, talented, and skillful at winning public office.

During her long life (1865-1961), Pauline was an Arizona State Legislator (1917-1921), she worked on presidential elections and she was involved in the suffrage movement. She was a temperance worker, a teacher, writer, artist, and businesswoman, along with a wife and mother.

Just nine years and three days after the event there was unveiled, yesterday July 3, 1907, on the courthouse plaza in the beautiful mountain Town of Prescott, whose mayor called home, and at the time he gave up his life for his country's flag, a beautiful equestrian statue, as a tribute to the memory of a man, who, today, is revered by every

Arizonan, and whose memory is kept in the hearts of all those who knew him in life. A fitting tribute and one well deserved.

As various speakers at yesterday's exercised extolled the virtues of Prescott's patriot, tears drilled the eyes of many; of those who had known him in the days gone by, and who had been proud to call him friend, along with a great pity welled lip in the hearts of the rugged Arizonans as he is no longer with us.

When the impressive draperies were pulled aside from Borglum's beautiful statue, it revealed the gallant captain, mounted on his charging horse. With distended nostrils the horse stands slightly reared back on his haunches, as though abruptly pulled up, while his rider, with face turned towards the left, sits in an attitude of expectancy, as though awaiting orders. It is a beautiful piece of craftsmanship, one well worthy of its subject.

Beneath the statue, forming its pedestal is a gigantic boulder, weighing twenty-eight tons, secured from one of the neighboring mountains, which Buckey loved so well in life. It remains in the rough, just as it was brought from the mountainside, carrying out the Rough Riders idea.

Many weary days were spent by Contractor H. C. Walter and his men, in transporting the boulder to its present resting place, it was tedious work, owing to the cumbrousness of the granite rock, but no work was too tedious for those who knew to what purpose the stone was to be put. Finally, it was embedded on a cement foundation in the city plaza, and all was in readiness for the mounting of the statue, which at that time had not yet arrived.

As time wore on and the statue, which was somewhere on the road on its way here from New York, did not arrive, grave fears were entertained that it would not arrive in time for the unveiling ceremonies to take place on the date arranged. Then it was demonstrated that railroads are not always the "soundest corporations" the big wigs like to picture themselves, and that a thread of sentiment, even like that which runs through the being's everyday mortals, is present also in the make-up of the directors of the railroad systems.

W. A. Drake, vice president of the Southern Pacific Railroad, was appealed to secure some trace of the statue and rush it through. He immediately set to work, and obtaining the cooperation of H. G. Wells of the coast lines of the Santa Fe, dispatched a special agent out on the road to look up the statue and rush it through at all hazard. This special agent was given the power to spare neither time nor expense in securing trace of the statue and getting it here on time. He found it buried in the yards at Albuquerque, New Mexico, and ordered it out on the first train leaving, in accordance with the orders of his superior officers. He rode with the train. At Winslow the car with the statue was located. It was sidelined for repairs. Ordinarily through the course of normal events the car would have been side tracked and had to wait for the next train. This was no ordinary occasion. However, the train was held several hours while all the mechanics obtainable were set to work repairing the car. At Ashfork a special engine was waiting to bring the car to Prescott, it arrived last

Saturday from Albuquerque in record time.

The work of mounting the statue on the pedestal was accomplished over the next two days, and yesterday the heroic bronze beauty was unveiled. Fitting it was that Maurice O'Neill, adopted son of the deceased hero, along with Miss Kitty Hickey, daughter of Buckey O'Neill's bosom friend in the days when the country was young, and history was warm in the making, should have been delegated as the persons to actually unveil the monument to the gaze of the populace.

With the unveiling aside, the beautiful bronze statue stood revealed, a mighty crow of hundreds that had assembled, with their hats off in respect for music, while the band played "America the Beautiful." Those present did homage to the memory of brave Buckey O'Neill.

On the following pages is a poem written by John Steven McGroarty, California poet, a famous historian, and dramatist of the passion play and the history of California. The poem was read aloud at the unveiling of the Roosevelt Rough Riders Equestrian Statue Depicting Captain William Owen Buckey O'Neill on the courthouse plaza at Prescott, July 3, 1907, which by the way just happened to be Armistice Day. The poem was recited by Miss Sharlot Hall, a local noted historian and celebrity, on the old capital grounds.

The Rough Riders

"Souls of rough riding men, the first born and the last, come and gather round us from out the storied past, come from the fields if

Monmouth, the red-dyed Bapidan, come with Putman and Marion, Stonewall and Sheridan, far from silent bivouacs that sleep in ancient dust, leap again to saddle; unsheathe your swords of rust, list to the bugle ringing clear on the desert sky, calling the war-worn trooper that no go ridding by.

Come and gather round us, souls of hard riding men, who fought with swinging sabers, of old, o'er hill and glen? Souls of strong adventurers, who blazed the bloody trail, down from the guns of Lexington to Shenandoah's vale; Halt your ghostly riders, your squadrons side by side, while they ride by who rode, as you, upon the battle's tide;

Wanderers of the savage hills and desert's blooming plain, who spilled their eager ears against the chivalry of Spain. We'll dream again they're gathered from near and far away, that at host to the Alamo rode down one sun-kissed day;

The bronco buster of the plains, the hunters from the hill. The keepers of the rainless washes that love and lure them brood of trackless wilderness swart with the deserts breath spawn of the deserts of the Southwest, whose trails are dim with death, we'll dream once more they're mustered, here beneath skies aglow. A thousand strong in the rendezvous, as then at the Alamo.

And as the dust-brown columns sweep on with the thunder, full will us filing a cheer for him, the chieftain at the head; A cheer for him, the chieftain, who led them on the way, at whose clear call to glory they galloped to the tray;

Him they trailed to glory where flamed the flag unfurled, the one great heart of all, best loved of the entire world; We'll lift our hearts to greet him as breaks the vision then, of Roosevelt still riding with his rough riding men. Sing from you throat, O bugle, as they ride forth at dawn, from Caney and Guaysimas and the long hill of San- Juan. Turn again, O Memory, with heart that holds them dear, again their steeds are champing the hoof-beats sounding near.

Home from the crimson fights they won, home they come at last, to ride in full review before the spirits of the past; Here, where one silent trooper waits upon the way, the last-rung trumpet call that wakes the Judgment Day.

Onward they come in full review, the living and the dead, troop and the plunging squadron, their leader at their head; and he will halt his charger while all the columns wheel where face to face they stand against Roosevelt and O'Neill. Up to the Colonel's lips will leap his saber in salute to him, the well- loved captain, who sits the stirrups mute, smiling as when he answered to freedom's crowding roll, and death flung darkness his wild and gallant soul.

So shall they come with memory from near and far away? The host that from the Alamo rode out on sunlit day, back they come to mountain and desert's shining plain, the living and the gloried dead, the wounded and the slain. Every saddle set once more as when they rode to war, to strike for a new republic, to die for a new born star; Not a gap in the ranks of dream that sailed the tropic sea, colonel, captains and troopers all home from Cuba free. They come and pass away as evening's shadow falls.

And good night songs and revile the singing bugle calls, leaving this one lone sentry upon the grime plateau over the purpled buttes aflame and shining dunes below. Here in the silent stirrups with desert stars agleam, soul of the wild adventure, heart of the deathless dream; One faithful sun-burned trooper that waits upon the way, the last-rung trumpet call that wakes the judgment day."

Rough Rider Buckey O'Neill

"When the cresset of war blazed over the land, and a call rang fierce through the west, saying, "Rough Rider, come to the roll of the drum!"

"They came with their bravest and best. With a clatter of hoofs and a stormy hail; Sinewy, lean and tall and brown;

Hunters and fighters and men of the trail, from hills and plains, from college and town; With the cowboy yell and Redman's whoop."

"Sons of thunder and swingers of steel; And, leading his own Arizona troop, rode glad and fearless Buckey O'Neill;"

"In the ranks there was Irish blood galore, as it ever is sure to be. When the Union flag is flung to the lore and the fight is to make men free."

"There were Kelly's, Murphy's and Burke's and Doyles. The colonel an Obrien strain and the lift of the race made a glow on each face, when they met on the Texan plain, but the man of them all with the iron will, man and soldier from the crown to heel."

"A leader and master in the games that kill, was soft voiced Captain Buckey O'Neill; On watch in the valley or charging the height, in a plunge cross the steep ravine, San-Juan or Las Guasimas, battle or fight, or a rush through the jungle screen, where the wave of the war took the battling host, the Rough Riders fronted the storm, and their dead on the rocker of red glory tossed, Amid spray with their life blood warm!"

"What wonder, then, holding his chivalrous vow, to stoop not, or crouch not, or kneel that death in hot anger struck full on the brow of dauntless Buckey O'Neill?"

"O battle that tries out the hearts of the strong, to your test he had answered true, who bent not his head and balked but at wrong, nor murmured what billet drew; In the cast of the terrible dice of doom, it came fair to his had as well, to mount the crest where the great laurels bloom, or to die at the foot where he fell, and of such are the victors and these alone shall be stamped with the hero seal and stirrup to stirrup they'll ride to the throne, from the colonel to Buckey O'Neill!"

On the following pages is the last poem that was read at Statue Dedication Ceremony for Buckey O'Neill's Rough Rider Statue before Governor McCord's ending speech. This poem was written by a Prescott citizen, by the name of George K. Powell.

GRAVE BY THE SIDE OF THE TRAIL

"The trails are forgotten, and covered with green are the paths now displaced by the rail? And only is left, where the white trains were seen, the lone grave by the side of the trail; The low little mound beneath a cushion of greens to mark the old overland trail!"

"Here, with life's hopes, lies a proud mother's joy, with no tablet to tell the dark tale, how her heart found a tomb, to sleep with her boy, in the grave by the side of the trail, to lie there eternal with far away boy, in the grave by the side of the trail!"

"The miner lies here, and the hunter you there as they fell for the warrior's fierce hail; With mission thus ended forevermore there in the grave by the side of the trail!"

"Here maiden was left on the way to the gold so legend is cut on the rail, and bowed was a head there, brave, manly and bold,"

"O'er the grave by the side of the trail; With bright hopes all buried, down deep beneath the mold, in the grave by the side of the trail!"

"But when the last trumpet, to rally again, is heard ringing mandate sublime, from peaks of the mountains to depths of the glen, down the paths of eternity's time Its music will miss then no mound long forgot, as it echoes through valley and vale, to reach amid the rest even the lone prairie spot with its grave by the side of the trail. To call him the lost one, in sorrow forgot, from the grave by the side of the trial!"

The above taken the day of the dedication of Buckey O'Neill's Roughrider statue was found in our National Archives

The following composition written by the widow of Prescott's famed "Buckey" O'Neill, first appeared in the San Francisco Examiner in 1898, shortly after O'Neill's death in the Spanish-American War as one of Theodore Roosevelt's Rough Riders. The exact date it appeared is not currently known, although the data undoubtedly exists somewhere.

Pauline O'Neill remembers Capt. Buckey O'Neill In her own words

"When the Maine was blown up and the whole nation was discussing the question of the war that might follow, Mr. O'Neill felt that his country would demand his services. A meeting was held here in the Courthouse on the evening following receipt of the news. Mr. O'Neill again declared that he was ready and willing to shed his heart's last drop for his flag, his country. He was then, as always, entirely devoid of fear. When the audience applauded his words, my heart sank, for I knew that in case of war, his honor would demand that he keep the promise so solemnly made to his fellowmen."

"Mr. O'Neill was always cheerful and happy at home, looking on the bright side of life on every occasion. He never wavered when he thought that duty called him to perform any task. Single-handed and alone, as Sheriff, he captured the hardest desperadoes. He was so gentle and kindhearted that he fainted at a hanging, because he saw the wife and children of the murderer who were left behind to be the by-word of an indignant populace. The wife was ill, and the children were so small and innocent that their future seemed an awful on to him."

"To me, he was always kind and loving, as much as lover in the last days as when he first courted me, twelve years ago. I held the first place in his heart always, for there were no living children who claimed a part of his love. To his adopted child, he has been more than a father, being a jolly comrade to the little fellow. He always wrote of the little child as the 'Wild Man from Borneo.'"

"Perhaps we were too happy, and that is why God saw fit to call him first?"

"Wives, mothers, sweethearts, and sisters of our gallant boys, write to your loved ones; write to them daily if possible; fill your letters with the small home incidents that go to make up life. Make the epistles cheerful. Keep the agony of your writing in your own hearts, even though they break, for our soldiers have enough to contend with outside of the sorrow and agony of the loved ones left behind."

"Every day since our marriage, when we were separated, I wrote a letter to my beloved, and he always wrote to me each day. Thus we were ever in touch with each other-no matter how far apart we were. His letters were sometimes short after he left, on May 4th, for San Antonio, for his duties as captain kept him busy from sunrise until midnight, but he always reported, as it were, with a few lines to let me know that he was well."

O'Neill, Circa 1898. This Photo was found in our National Pauline Archives

"You ask me if I gave him up willingly to fight for our flag. No, thousand times, no. Do we give up our heart's blood, or our children, or our loved ones willingly? We, women of this world? Can we say 'Go,' when we feel there is no coming back in this world? Is it to be expected that we shall say, like the Spartan mother, 'Return with your shield, or on it'? You men who clamored for war, did you know what it would mean to the women of our country, when the shouts of victory would be ineffectually drown the moans of the women who mourned for the lives of those that were given to make that victory possible?"

"With these stern realities, can we make this sacrifice willingly? We would be less human and more divine if we could cheerfully say, 'Yes,' to a sacrifice that breaks our hearts and makes dreary and sorrowful the rest of our days."

"Until he received his commission, I would not believe that he was in earnest. He joked and laughed about going, I thought that the idea that he was needed had left him. On the 28th of April, he returned from Phoenix with his captaincy in his pocket, and the following day he was mustered in, the first volunteer in the whole United States to offer his services and his life, if need be, to his country. From that day on, my heart began to break, although made no sigh."

"I went to the train on May 4th to see the gallant Rough Riders leave. My eyes were tearless, while my heart was wrung in agony-at the last good-bye, he said, 'my dear, the war will not last long, and I will return in ninety days.' But my heart kept repeating, 'Forever, forever!'"

"From that day on, the silver threads have crept into my hair, while my face has become hollow and old from worry and grief."

"Yet, despite my feelings, I have always endeavored to be cheerful in all of my letters, only occasionally letting my feelings reveal themselves. He, too, though he felt lonely and homesick, disguised his words. In one of his last letters, he even planned to have me visit him in Havana next winter."

"The last letter I received was written the day after the first fight, June 26th. It was short and only written to let me know that he was still unharmed. He had to make the letter brief, because he wanted to help bury the dead."

"When the news of the next battle came, I was out of town, in a neighboring city, on business. Fortunately, the telegram did not reach me until I stepped off the train, when kind hands and loving hearts led me home. The agony was so great that I could not weep for days. The agony was so great that I could not weep for days. Later reports say that he fell, killed instantly, as he was leading his men to victory. A second before he went to his death, he said to one of the boys that the Spanish bullet was not made that could kill him."

"And so it all ended, of what use is the Medal of Honor that he was to have for trying to rescue the two soldiers, of what use the praise and the laurels, the undying glory of being a nation's hero, the thanks of a grateful country-of what use to me, who has lost the most precious being of my life?"

"Yet I am not alone, for thousands weep with me, and refuse to be comforted, while thousands of others are still waiting and praying that the dread news will not come to them."

"To you who will celebrate our nation's success, when your spirits are raised in triumph and your songs of thanksgiving are the loudest, remember that we, who sit and weep in our closed and darkened homes, have given our best gifts to our country and our flag. Patriotism, how many hearts are broken in thy cause?"

The following is the official Governments official report on Captain William Owen Buckey O'Neill's military record:

"Buckey O'Neill was the first to offer his service to his country in the Spanish-American War. He resigned as Mayor of Prescott and immediately began to form a cavalry regiment of Arizona men. To show the respect he had at the time he was able to enroll over 1,000 men, however, only 210 had been allotted to Arizona."

"Buckey O'Neill was made the rank of captain, and on May 4, 1898, the men assembled at Fort Whipple Barracks after a show of support from the City of Prescott, and left by train to San Antonio, Texas, for their initial training."

"In San Antonio, he was given command of Troop A, which became part of the First United States Volunteer Cavalry. A remark by Colonel Theodore Roosevelt, who was to be the leader in charge to a newspaper

reporter saying, he was going to Texas to join a regiment of rough riding men gave the name that has gone down in history. From then on, the regiment was called "Roosevelt's Rough Riders."

"To Buckey O'Neill, it was a short but meteoric path from Mayor of Prescott to San-Juan Hill. It was there that he was fatally wounded on July 1, 1898. One year later, on May 1, 1899, Buckey O'Neill was laid to rest with the nation's honored dead at Arlington National Cemetery. Exactly nine years from the anniversary of his death, a bronze statue was dedicated to his memory at the Courthouse Plaza in his home town of Prescott, Arizona."

The burial of Captain O'Neill Washington, D.C., May 1, 1899

"The body of Captain William Owen O'Neill of the Rough Riders was interred at Arlington National Cemetery today. He was buried just in front of the grave of Captain Allyn Capron who, like Captain O'Neill, lost his life in the Santiago campaign, namely in the assault on San-Juan Hill."

I think the statement I like best is the last sentence on the monument that was spoken to

Teddy Roosevelt by Buckey O'Neill when he first met the future President, which was carved into his monument and really sums up the grit and patriotism of Captain Buckey O'Neill. The wording on the monument follows:

WILLIAM OWEN O'NEILL
Mayor of Prescott, Arizona,

Capt. Troop A, First U.S. Vol. Cav. Rough Riders
Brevet Major Born February 2, 1860
Killed July 1, 1898, At San-Juan Hill, Cuba
"Who would not die for a new star on the flag?"

Ode to Buckey O'Neill
By Zeke Crandall

Bucking the Tiger is how you got your name
But it was not what brought you fame

Together with St. Clair, Black, Holton and Horn
You chased the Canyon Diablo Robbers till
you were torn

You cornered the gang in Whaweap Canyon
While your men rested at a camp near
the town of Manyon

You held them at bay till your men caught up
Then you and your posse took them home to
pay up

You were such a young sheriff,
just barely taken your oath
Your men followed their leader
through rain and snow

National fame came to you from this
monumental pursuit
From Mayor to Captain in your
striking suit

You gave your life at San-Juan Hill
To preserve our freedom, you imposed
your will

All Arizona thanks you for bravery
and your plight
Your writing brought us fame, you
were a pure delight

BIBLIOGRAPHY

Sharlot Hall Museum Archives,
Prescott, Arizona.

Arizona Train Robbers, written by Zeke Crandall, published in 2006.

Ghost in the Desert, written by Zeke Crandall, published in 2008.

The Death Cave, written by Zeke Crandall, published in 2012.

The Camel Corp, written by Zeke Crandall, published in 2014.

Buckey O'Neill of the Southwest,
Arizona Highways article by Mauchline Muir.

Apaches and Longhorns, written by Will Barnes, autobiography, published in 1941.

The Arizona Weekly Journal-Miner Newspaper,
Various articles author has on file.

The Phoenix Herald Newspaper,
Various articles author has on file.

The San Francisco Examiner Newspaper,
Various articles various articles author owns.

The Prescott Courier Newspaper,
Various articles author has on file.

Taming the Frontier, Arizona Highways Magazine, by William MaCloed Raine

Yavapai County Records Division, official transcripts by William Buckey O'Neill, Yavapai County Sheriff and Tax Assessor.

The Williams News- Historical Article by Dean John R. Murdock, Professor of History.

Rough Riders - Buckey O'Neill of Arizona written by Dale L. Walker.

Railroads of Arizona, Volume 4, written by David Myrick.

The Requiem of the Drum, Cosmopolitan Magazine, February, 1901, article written by William Owen O'Neill.

The Arizona Historical Society, Flagstaff Branch, Joe Meehan, Archivist.

Wolf Trading Post, Canyon Diablo and Two Guns history articles written by Gladwell Richardson, several Arizona newspapers and magazines.

Famous Sheriffs and Western Outlaws, by William MacLoed Raine, Skyhorse Publishing, New York, New York, page 87-88. (1903, republished in 2012)

The Daily Picanune Newspaper, an article published in New Orleans, Louisiana, April 11, 1889.

About the Author;

William "Tom" Vyles aka Zeke Crandall was born in London, Ontario, Canada. The family moved to Phoenix, Arizona in 1956. A life long battle with Asthma, several bouts with pneumonia, in an out of hospitals the first nine years of life, the family was instructed by physicians to move to Arizona for the hot dry climate.

In and out of school until age ten, home schooled by his mother Elizabeth, reading "The Books of Knowledge," encyclopedia, Tom fell in love with history. With no family in Arizona, our family adopted elderly neighbors, Kenny and Mary Harris, as our Arizona grandparents.

Kenny worked in the stockyards in Cincinnati as a brand inspector for cattle coming from Arizona. He became friends of John Wayne, who brought his cattle through the stockyards in Cincinnati. John talked Kenny into moving to Arizona. Kenny was a professional fiddle player, along with his friend Rudy MacDonald, who played banjo, they toured Arizona playing gigs.

Young Tom went along on most of the out of town music gigs. His job was to set up instruments and equipment. The carrot for Tom was that Kenny would take him rabbit and quail hunting the next day. Young Tom fell in love with Arizona history, because Kenny introduced him to many amazing older men, who told him stories of the old west.

Other current books are available by this author through our website, www.arizonatales.com, by email, zekecrandall46@hotmail.com or call (602) 399-1811 for special pricing and shipping costs.

www.ingramcontent.com/pod-product-compliance
Lightning Source LLC
Chambersburg PA
CBHW070647160426
43194CB00009B/1607